Contents

Preface

In *The Art Of The Beatles* I have attempted to explore more fully the subject matter and theme of the exhibition of the same name, presented by Merseyside County Council at the Walker Art Gallery, Liverpool, from May to September 1984. The Beatles' influence on popular music is well documented, but their impact on the world of visual arts – on photography, painting, graphic design, cinema etc. – has hardly been considered. The exhibition was the first attempt to bring together as much significant visual material related to the Beatles as possible. In doing so, it became apparent that the material was so abundant – and of such interest in its own right – that the exhibition and the accompanying catalogue could not do full justice to the subject. It was decided, therefore, that there should be a permanent commemoration of the event, in the form of an illustrated book that would stand as a lasting record of the Beatles' importance to the visual culture of the second half of the 20th century.

The Beatles' heyday lasted only from 1963 to 1970, but during that time they became the most important single element in British popular culture of the post-war years.

Views of the cultural growth (some would say decline) of Britain over the past quarter century use the Beatles as landmarks of that process. Their emergence was symptomatic of a new indigenous youth movement, independent of the American-based teenage culture of the 1950s; their success was part of, and came to signify, the "swinging 'sixties", for better or for worse; their swift demise, in retrospect, has come to echo the sudden change from optimism to pessimism in the recession years of the 1970s. Since then, their omnipresence as a symbol of an era has reinforced the "nostalgic" view of recent history, and has convincingly demonstrated the astonishing durability of both the Beatles' music and their image.

Their appeal was, from the start, visual almost as much as musical. Their image was always unique. Unlike their contemporaries on the music scene, whose style *reflected* the times, the Beatles invariably helped to *establish* fashion – and not just fashion in clothes. Photography, graphics, illustration, advertising – all influenced, and were influenced by, the image of the Beatles.

It would be naive to suggest that the Beatles were stylistic innovators in the cretive sense. Even where they were most genuinely artistic, in their music, they admitted that they were frequently no more than inspired jackdaws – borrowers and adaptors. It was in their ability to sense and utilise elements of visual style, so that they became part of their own image, that the Beatles ensured that they were uniquely recognisable from the very beginning, and have remained so ever since.

In identifying the variety of manifestations of that image, *The Art Of The Beatles* aims to trace the origins and impact of the visual style of the Beatles, an essential aspect of their career and its influence over the past twenty years.

The exhibition, and subsequently this book, would not have been possible without the support and participation of Merseyside County Council, the director and staff of the Walker Art Gallery, all those who contributed material and advice, and – especially – Merseyside Tourism Devlopment Officer, Ron Jones, whose concept the exhibition first was.

Nor would any of this have occurred were it not for the original influence and inspiration of the Beatles, past and present.

Mike Evans, May 1984

People and Things that Went Before

The popular culture of the twentieth century has been dominated by strong visual images. In an age that produced those most visual of media, the cinema and television, this is hardly surprising – and indeed it was the cinema that for decades produced the strongest of these images. Almost everyone in the world could recognize Charlie Chaplin, just by the emblem of his hat and cane: the image was truly universal. The same could be said of Shirley Temple or Marilyn Monroe, and of many others.

The cinema created modern day icons, instantly recognizable symbols of real people, and when music became the predominant "pop" medium from the mid '50s, it too (although not an essentially visual form) thrived on image and visual style.

Towering above all others in the late '50s, straddling the stage and guitar slung low, was the image of Elvis Presley, the personification of the spirit of rock'n'roll. Elvis represented the American dream come true, truck driver to millionaire overnight, but for a few short years he also represented the restlessness and rebellion of youth, embodying the teenage view of the romance of America. It was an image that was particularly potent for the teenagers of mid-'50s England, still a seemingly grey place only a couple of years past ration books and post-war austerity, and provided a romantic perspective that was fundamental in shaping the style and image that was to dominate "pop" culture through the next decade and beyond, the era of the Beatles.

Although its days as a major port were already numbered by the late 1950s, physically Liverpool had changed little from its commercial heyday earlier in the century. Behind the grand opulence of shipping lines' and insurance companies' offices along the pierhead waterfront – the first sight to greet thousands of transatlantic passengers on their arrival in England – lay a maze of towering warehouses intersecting the main thoroughfares of the city centre. This in turn gave way to the wide streets of Georgian houses, once the homes of the merchant middle classes, named after those same merchants and politicians – Huskisson, Canning, Abercrombie – as the majestic docks they overlooked. Beyond, to the south, the leafy suburbs; east and north from the inner city, mile after mile of Victorian "two-up and two-down" working class streets.

The demolition of the worst slums of the latter had already begun, as more and more families resettled from inner city Everton or Dingle to the new industrial estates of Kirkby, Croxteth and Cantrill Farm. The grand town houses of the merchant gentry, on the other hand, had provided for another kind of resettlement, becoming the natural habitat of the immigrant, the itinerant and the bohemian. By 1958, the north end of Liverpool 8 (now better known as Toxteth) from Princes Park to the Gothic splendour of the new Anglican Cathedral, was host to a unique community of new immigrant families, descendants of seamen of all nations, artists, students, poets and prostitutes. It was here, within walking distance of the University, the Philharmonic Hall and the College of Art, that most of the new cultural activity of the city flourished.

Geographically, Liverpool 8 was the environment of key elements in the Beatles' early stylistic development, but for the roots of that development we have to go back to the schoolboy fascination with the rock'n'roll dream.

Cynthia Lennon: Family groups. These poster-colour portraits, done in the 1980s, show the Beatles with their families set against their respective Liverpool homes. By way of a romantic rather than realistic slant, the Royal Liver Building appears in the background of each painting.

John

Paul

George

Ringo

All These Places Had Their Moments

Like the rest of England, Liverpool was subject to the onslaught of the mid-'50s explosion of rock'n'roll. Between '55 and '57 a new assertive youth culture came to the fore, heralded by movies like *Rebel without a Cause* (with James Dean), *The Wild One* (Marlon Brando) and *Blackboard Jungle* – the last scoring a double impact in that it tied the new teenage rebellion firmly to emergent rock'n'roll by featuring Bill Haley's *Rock Around The Clock* in its opening sequence. With the enormous influence of Haley, Presley and the rest came a whole *style* based on rock'n'roll, an essentially *American* style.

Although the classic Teddy Boys had appeared in England a couple of years prior to rock, it was the "punk" (in the pre-1970s sense of the word) image of Dean and Presley that took over after 1955, and from then on, the "Ted" mixed Edwardian drapes with bootlace ties and blue jeans. A hybrid mix of English (the narrow "drainpipe" trousers, particularly, were always regarded as a curiosity by Americans) and American styles had evolved, seized upon by teenage rock'n'roll fans across the country

The fresh-faced Lennon and cherubic McCartney were no exceptions, as the earliest pictures of the erstwhile skifflers as The Quarrymen reveal. Together with the younger George Harrison, they adopted the mode of dress most frowned upon by grammar school headmasters – and they were all grammar school pupils at the time. To paraphrase George Melly, revolt became style; in this case, the revolt was against the conservative values of school and family life, the style – rock'n'roll.

Of the schoolboy Beatles-to-be, John Lennon was the most "artistic" in the visual sense. His only claim to fame as a pupil at Quarry Bank Grammar School were the notorious (and now legendary) *Daily Howl* caricatures he produced of fellow pupils and members of the staff. After passing no O-levels in his GCE exam, there ended what could only be called an undistinguished school career, to be followed by an equally chequered – but far

Paul McCartney: McCartney has demonstrated a life-long interest in Rupert Bear, even to the extent of acquiring the rights to the character. These doodles date back to his childhood in the mid-'40s.

Anne Mason: The only known portrait of John Lennon during his art school days. Anne Mason was in the same year as John, and a close friend of Cynthia Powell.

Keen Type.

Not so keen types.

Rod Murray/Cynthia Lennon

Dad's just not awake until he's had his Shwedded Feet.

This is not Robert Mitchum

Rod Murray/Cynthia Lennon

John Lennon: Pages from his *Daily Howl*, passed on to fellow student Rod Murray when Lennon vacated their communal Gambier Terrace flat.

more stimulated – studentship at Liverpool College of Art.

The art schools in the late '50s represented most conspicuously the other stream of British youth culture – that of the "student" type, the beatnik and the pseudo-existentialist. Altogether a more "middle class" pose, rooted in the grammar schools, it nevertheless stood for a classless attitude and a rebellion against bourgeois values far stronger than that represented by rock'n'roll (which was basically a rebellion about age rather than social values).

Youthful bohemianism in Britain was identified by duffle coats and beards, ban-the-bomb marches, an elementary dabbling in soft drugs, and an enthusiasm for jazz and the American "beat" writers.

Lennon, the quasi-Ted, steeped by now in the material and mythology of rock'n'roll music, despising students with their beards and sandals, half-baked philosophy and archaic jazz, was still the odd man out. Yet he *was* an art student, not a truck driver like his hero Elvis, and what certainly rubbed off was the liberating influence of the artistic environment.

One of Lennon's tutors at the Art College was Arthur Ballard, who recalls that his work was remarkable in that it was virtually non-existent – "When it came time for the students' work to be displayed around the walls at the end of term, John Lennon was the only student I have ever known to have other members of the class cover up for him by displaying *their* work as his."However, Ballard's opinion of Lennon's ability was modified when he came across John's cartoons for the first time. "One day I found this notebook, full of caricatures…the wittiest things I'd ever seen" – which convinced him that Lennon's talent was as a purveyor of surreal humour rather than in "serious" art.

Lennon's career at Liverpool is remembered by those around at the time as a constant stream of nonsense humour, cruel send-ups and drunken bouts – of which stories are legion – in anarchic sessions in the art students pub Ye Cracke.

Images Of Broken Light

It was in the Cracke in 1958 that Lennon was introduced to Stuart Sutcliffe by fellow student Bill Harry, an event that was to influence him profoundly in the coming months. In many ways the two couldn't have been more different; Sutcliffe small, quiet and already a painter of considerable potential. "He had an amazing energy, an intensity…throwing all his enthusiasm into vast works, huge canvasses" Arthur Ballard remembers "…yet he was sensitive to the point of not painting with the rest of his year in College…I used to visit him for private tutorials in his basement studio". The basement in question was one of a series of rooms shared with Rod Murray, another student at the college, culminating in a notorious flat at 3 Gambier Terrace which Lennon also shared, and which featured in an expose in *The People* newspaper as an example of the "Beatnik horror" sweeping the country!

Himself a painter whose work had moved towards the abstract during the late '50s, Ballard actively encouraged Sutcliffe's talent while teaching him in his first (Intermediate course) year at Liverpool. Sutcliffe, however, was not so fortunate when he moved into the mainstream of his studentship, for the National Diploma of Design.

The English art schools of the period, whilst being fertile ground for student eccentricity and rebellion, were in many ways still a bastion of academic conservativism. Much of the tuition was based on English art of the 1930s and '40s, but in the "real world" outside, particularly in America, the old artistic barriers – like the musical and literary barriers of the time – were being shattered.

The abstract expressionists, Jackson Pollock, Mark Rothko and the rest of the New York school, and their English counterparts of the early and middle '50s, were already giving way to the new "pop" painters like Jasper Johns and Robert Rauschenburg. Indeed, the artistic ghetto of Liverpool 8 reflected these developments; abstract painting proliferated in the work, among others, of Ballard, John Edkins and Don McKinlay, while aspects of "pop" were emerging in the painting of Adrian Henri and Sam Walsh – the first two painters to feature the Beatles in their work a few years later.

At Liverpool, Sutcliffe's work was constantly in conflict with the current formalities of art school tuition, particularly when he entered the National Diploma of Design course after completing the Intermediate. His two tutors in composition were George Meyer Martin and Nicholas Horsfield; Horsfield recognises now that, at the time, he was attempting to teach Sutcliffe in a style based on the 1930s, which was totally inappropriate to a student like Stuart in the late 1950s…."I saw a brittleness in his tonality, tried to get him to reach for better harmony, but I was teaching something valid in the '30s and '40s…..I didn't impede him, but was not able to guide him in the way that Paolozzi eventually was".

His work constantly challenged the conventions of the art school method of the time. "His painting never toed the line, but was limited by the system" recalls Horsfield, who went on to refuse Sutcliffe a reference for a teaching course after he had gained his diploma – "basically because I always discouraged really *able* artists from teachers' training – Stuart was an artist and nothing else."

Cynthia Lennon

Cynthia Lennon: "E-aar gerl.....how much?" From her *Twist Of Lennon* biography of 1978, Cynthia Lennon recalls her transformation from suburban to "bohemian" fashion under the influence of boyfriend John.

Life Is Very Short...

Pauline Sutcliffe

Stuart Sutcliffe: Self-portrait; oil on canvas, c. 1959.

What Sutcliffe and Lennon did have in common was that basically they were both romantics; Lennon nurturing the image of a tough no-nonsense rock'n'roller, Sutcliffe the transatlantic bohemianism of the new American beat writers. As their friendship developed, their conversation took in Ginsberg and Ferlinghetti as well as painters from Van Gogh to Jackson Pollock – Sutcliffe stimulating Lennon with his enthusiasm, Lennon implanting the romantic image of rock'n'roll musician in Sutcliffe's mind when the embryo Beatles asked him to play bass with them.

Already gaining a reputation as a painter, Stuart sold a painting for £60 at the prestigious John Moores Exhibition at Liverpool's Walker Art Gallery, with which he bought a bass guitar. No musician of any merit, Sutcliffe nevertheless made a significant impact on the early visual style of the Beatles with his own brand of rock'n'roll image, somewhere between a beatnik and a Teddy Boy, affecting the "mean and moody" stance of screen actor James Dean, already a posthumous cult figure. During a brief period when the group decided to adopt *noms de plumes*, Sutcliffe, the constant romantic, even dubbed himself "Stu de Staël" after painter Nicholas de Staël who also died in tragic circumstances early in his life.

It was Sutcliffe, again following a penchant for *la vie bohême*, who introduced the group to local entrepreneur Alan Williams. Williams was a lively character on the fringe of Liverpool 8 bohemia; he organised a riotous "arts ball" to rival the London Chelsea Arts Ball, employing Stuart and John to manipulate a float down Lime Street to the venue, St George's Hall; he went on to open the club which became a social catalyst for the Merseybeat scene, the Blue Angel. But at the time of Stuart's introducing him to the others, he was the proprietor of an "arty" coffee bar, the Jacaranda. Here Stuart would spend his non-painting hours lounging around, usually with Lennon. The place had the right tatty ambience ("candle-in-bottle style" Williams was to describe it years later) for

Pauline Sutcliffe

Astrid Kirchherr: Stuart Sutcliffe during his James Dean period.

the garret-artist life-style Stuart emulated, and when he wanted a wall decorated in the basement club of "the Jac", Williams hired Sutcliffe and his cronies to do the job. "End of the world, ban-the-bomb stuff" was how Alan Williams summed it up. Legend had it for years that the mural was the work of Sutcliffe and Lennon, but when it was "discovered" with the removal of a wooden facade recently, controversy raged, with fellow students of the period Bill Harry and Rod Murray insisting that neither Beatle had actually had a hand in the newly exposed painting.

By this time, the Silver Beatles, as they had become known (after changing their name from Johnny and the Moondogs) had begun to look like a group, with black polo-neck sweaters, black jeans and white plimsolls – but not like the mohair-suited norm of English "pop" groups of the period. So Williams decided to book them for the Jacaranda, as a change from the regular West

Indian steel band.

Subsequently Williams, acting as *de facto* manager of the group, fixed them other jobs – around Merseyside, on a tour of Scotland and, most importantly, in Hamburg.

The Hamburg experience was as crucial in the development of the Beatles' image as in the effect that it had on their music. The latter has been well documented; suffice to say here that the first five-month stint of Hamburg club hours provided a tough apprenticeship out of which the group emerged a musically matured outfit.

...And There's No Time

Stuart Sutcliffe: Self-portrait, 1961; the first ever picture of a Beatle "mop top", taken immediately after the historic haircut.

Pauline Sutcliffe

In the German sea port of Hamburg, based in the red light district of St Pauli around the notorious Reeperbahn, the Beatles yet again fell in with the artistic fringes of society; almost immediately, they were adopted by a group of students from the local art college, self-styled intellectuals dabbling in the *avant garde*, be it literature, art or merely life-style. The three who most prominently attached themselves to the Beatles were photographer Jurgen Vollmer, musician/artist Klaus Voorman and his girlfriend, the enigmatic Astrid Kirchherr, also studying photography. Astrid became hypnotised by the Beatles' animal charisma, and very soon became the girlfriend of Stuart Sutcliffe.

Astrid's influence on the appearance of the Beatles (they dropped the "Silver" soon after their first Hamburg trip) was incalculable. She took photographs of them constantly, moody black and white studies that were to set the tone for the way their image developed over the next five or six years. She encouraged them to wear black leather, and it was Astrid who was responsible for their eventual adoption of flat "art student" hair styles. Just as the teddy boy look was out of step in Liverpool College of Art, so the flat haircuts favoured by art students were against the grain in the greased-back world of early '60s rock musicians. Astrid cut Stuart's hair, and George's, in mid-1961, and they were followed soon by John and Paul, courtesy of Jurgen Vollmer.

Astrid was undoubtedly an influence on Stuart's leaving the group. He never developed his bass guitar playing to any degree, and sometimes only Lennon's loyalty kept him his place in the Beatles; yet on other occasions his lack of ability would make him the butt of the cruel streak in Lennon's humour. Astrid encouraged him in his painting, and he left the group in 1961 to enrol full time at the Hamburg State Art College under Eduardo Paolozzi. By the end of the year he was suffering from increasing attacks of headaches, culminating in a fatal brain haemorrhage in April 1962.

During the few months he studied with Paolozzi,

Sutcliffe produced a frantic explosion of work in a much more personal style than he had been able to achieve at Liverpool. In his analysis of the visual artists of Liverpool in *Art In a City* (1967), John Willett wrote of Sutcliffe:

"Probably no recent Liverpool painter has worked with anything resembling this intensity, and the range, variety and colour of his last few months' works made a very strong impression when they were shown at the Walker Art Gallery in May 1964.....he was an outstanding loss to Liverpool and quite possibly to English painting. And over and above the merit of his pictures he has a special significance as somebody whose burning creativity switched from art into pop music and then back again. He showed the way."

Pauline Sutcliffe

Stuart Sutcliffe: Hamburg painting, 1961.

In The Town Where I Was Born

After their first couple of visits to Hamburg, during 1961, the Beatles' image really began to develop. Aided by some of Astrid's photography and the black leather and t-shirts look they had now adopted permanently, they were aquiring a local following back in Liverpool. Indeed, at their first Merseyside appearance after the first five-month Hamburg visit, being advertised as "direct from Hamburg", the audience assumed they were German: but not for long – they built up a solid Liverpool support on a scene that, by the beginning of 1962, was 'boasting over two hundred full-time beat groups.

A glance at the pages of a vintage *Merseybeat*, the local music paper founded by Bill Harry, tells us something about the Beatles' style of dress. While they were in their invariable black leather, the rest of the groups featured looked like The Shadows – sharp suits, Tony Curtis haircuts; tatty flash as opposed to the Beatles' flashy tat.

As their reputation grew, so did the demand for photographs. Until they signed with Brian Epstein late in 1961, much of the photo' material aquired by their growing army of followers was "bootlegged" copies of pictures by Astrid and (to a lesser extent) Paul McCartney's brother Mike.

Mike, Paul's junior by two years, worked in a Liverpool hairdressers in the early '60s, but exhibited a talent with the camera never fully exploited. His photographs of the Beatles between 1961 and 1963 represent a rare historic archive by one on the "inside", and fine photographs in their own right. He recorded the Beatles at home – Paul and John crouched over guitars in the McCartney house, midway through writing *I Saw Her Standing There* for instance – the Beatles on gigs at the Cavern and elsewhere, and the Beatles relaxing. Years later, recalling the demand for McCartney's photographs by the fans, one-time Cavern regular Pat Dawson confessed "We used to pester Mike McCartney something wicked for photographs…"

The Beatles commanded a local fan loyalty similar to that generated by Liverpool and Everton football clubs. The front row of seats at the Cavern

Anonymous: Snap taken by a fan, c. 1962, typical of hundreds passed around by the Beatles' Liverpool following.

acquired such a premium when the Beatles were playing – although they played there four or five times a week – that it was not unknown for the hard core of followers to queue all night in the dank Mathew Street doorway just to secure the exclusive positions the following evening.

Much of the fans' identification with the Beatles was on an image level, to the extent that they began adopting the Beatles' dress and style to their own (mainly female) requirements – suede waistcoats, leather jackets, tab collar shirts – a phenomenon unknown for a group with no media hype or exposure. The longest-standing female fans had adopted a hairstyle more often associated with art students in the early '60s: long, straight and black, usually with pale lipstick – although their office and factory work-mates favoured the currently popular "beehive" style. In an even more extreme display of devotion, some of the local fans had their hair cut short and flat in direct imitation of the group.

The ease with which the Beatles' mode of dress could be adapted by the opposite sex demonstrated the asexual nature of some fashion developments to come rather than any sexual ambiguity in the wearers. Within eighteen months these seemingly local eccentricities of style, among otherwise ordinary working class girls, would be the fashion across the country.

Mike McCartney: John and Paul with Gene Vincent at the Cavern. ☛

Mike McCartney

Mike McCartney: Shoe shop.

Mike McCartney: "Rogers and Hammersmith at work".

Mike McCartney: "John, Paul, George and Dennis" – probably the first ever colour photograph of the Beatles.

Mike McCartney: Backstage looning with John, Paul, Pete and George. ☛

May I Introduce To You

igning with Brian Epstein in late 1961 heralded two major steps in the evolution of the image of the Beatles. That they were potently photogenic was evident in the work of Vollmer, Kirchherr and the younger McCartney, but no photographic sessions had been organised on a formalised basis until Bill Harry's *Merseybeat* newspaper began commissioning local photographers – Dick Mathews, Don Valentine, Graham Spencer and Harry Wattmough among them – to take pictures of the group. The deal Harry offered usually included free advertising in the paper, a name credit on each photograph and his willingness to "put work their way" through

groups' managers and so on. And out of this arrangement, through 1962, came a series of pictures that was to put a definitive stamp on the visual identity of the Beatles.

The crucial photographs were done through Bill Connell's Peter Kaye agency, and were the work of Les Chadwick. an ex-colleague of Harry's from his days at the Junior Art School. Although the earlier sessions – while Pete Best was still drummer with the group – reflected the black leather look that was becoming a Beatles trademark, pictures after Ringo Starr became a Beatle in the summer of 1962 signified Brian Epsteins famous move to "smarten" up the group's appearance. Apparently

Peter Kaye

Les Chadwick: Before: the "leather" Beatles.

against the immediate instincts of the Beatles, especially John Lennon, Epstein persuaded them to don neat Italian-style box jacket suits, shirts and ties, and cord waistcoats, on stage at the Cavern. But somehow they still managed to look unlike the rest of the Liverpool groups. While the Beatles were anticipating fashion that was to take over in the wake of their success in a few months time, Merseybeat style by and large was still the mohair and lame norm of '62 "pop".

While most of Chadwick's work for Merseybeat featured the Beatles in the live gig situation, at the Cavern and elsewhere, a series of location shots commissioned – on Bill Harry's suggestion – by Brian Epstein emphasised the gritty edge to their personality and music. The juxtaposition of the almost clean-cut image with scenes of urban dereliction gives the pictures a special place in the history of the Beatles' image; the famous "bomb-site" settings were Epstein's idea, against flaking walls and burnt out cars, and the Liverpool cityscape of ferry boats, warehouses and the Royal Liver Building at the pierhead.

Don Valentine: Already aware of the importance of the media, the Beatles being interviewed for local hospital radio backstage at Hulme Hall, Port Sunlight, October 1962.

Les Chadwick: After: the "collar and tie" Beatles.

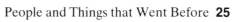

Peter Kaye

Les Chadwick: Bombsite

Les Chadwick: Bombsite.

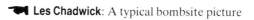 **Les Chadwick**: A typical bombsite picture

Peter Kaye

Try To See It My Way

Perhaps the most significant factor in the image of the Beatles in 1962 – and financial considerations had a certain amount to do with it – was that it was almost exclusively black-and-white. Most pop group photography was, of course, but whereas most pop acts "put up" with monochrome until they could afford the dubious luxury of the Cliff Richard technicolour record sleeve style of pictures, the Beatles' photographers consistently exploited the black-and-white medium for its own sake. From the Hamburg pictures of Vollmer and Kirchherr to the straight fan photos of Les Chadwick – all heralded in their own way the "grainy" style of black-and-white realism that became a dominant feature of the Beatles' image for years to come, and of much in '60s photography generally.

So before the Beatles had even had a record

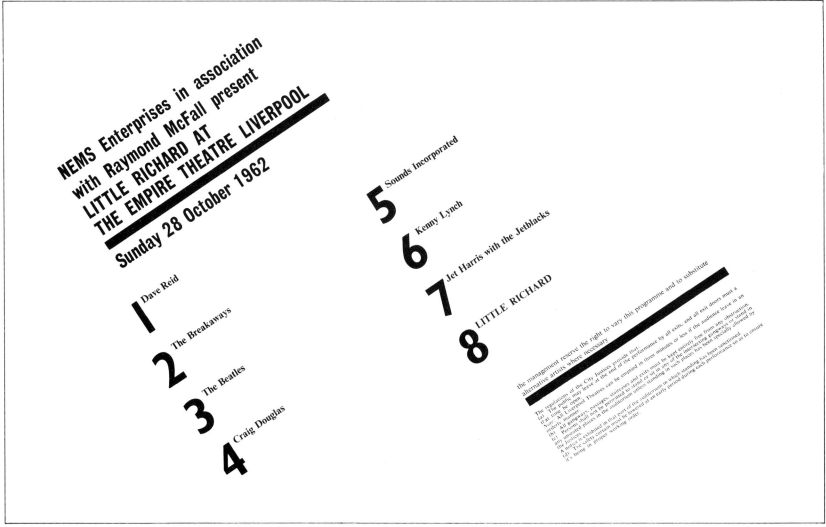

Programme for a little Richard concert at the Liverpool Empire, October 1962.....

THE BEATLES

John Lennon

George Harrison

Paul MaCartney

Ringo Starr

John, Paul and George met when at school in 1956 and have remained together ever since. They have played as a group with numerous names, various drummers and other augmentations. Their present drummer, Ringo Starr, has only recently joined the group but they have admired and known him since their schooldays.

1962 has been an exciting and important year for **The Beatles**. They have spread their wings and their appearances in many different parts of the country have always effected the same result . . . an invitation to return. They have made three broadcasts on the Light Programme in Peter Pilbeam's 'Teenagers Turn'. Granada T.V. filmed the group at the Cavern Club, Liverpool. They play at the Cavern (in the heart of the city) sometimes as many as three times a week, often a mid-day session . . . always it's a full house.

In May they were the principal attraction to open the fantastically successful Star-Club in Hamburg. Whilst they were away their manager took tapes to A. & R. Manager George Martin who subsequently signed them for Parlophone records. Both sides of their first single have been written by Paul and John. 'Love Me Do' was written in 1958 (in the skiffle days) and P.S. I Love You' was written whilst the group was playing in Germany at the Star-Club.

.....with photographs by Astrid Kirchherr. These were the first side-lit portrait photographs, predating Robert Freeman's by 18 months.

Terry O'Hara

Tex O'Hara: Sketches for "Beetle" drumskin logo.

released nationally – apart from some early Hamburg sides never promoted in England – they had an established image; an image that consisted of flat haircuts and cuban heeled boots, tab collar shirts and short jackets, set in grimy landscapes and sweating beat clubs – an image that even included their drumskin logo (the work of Terry O'Hara) featuring a beetle's antennae on the "B".

Most potently, it was an image that reflected, and echoed in the common consciousness, the varied facets of the pop style of the previous half dozen years – beatniks and Teddy Boys, coffee bars and cellar clubs, neat "mod" suits and (for the time) long hair. It was an image waiting to be developed by the Beatles and those around them, when they first found national fame – which, at the end of 1962, was just around the corner.

Peter Kaye

Les Chadwick: On stage at the Cavern.

GREAT NEWS OF "THE BEATLES"

THE BEATLES   Photograph by Alan Swerdlow

In our last issue we promised our readers some exciting news about The Beatles. This is it: Impresario Brian Epstein informs Mersey Beat that he has secured a recording contract with the powerful E.M.I. organisation for The Beatles to record for the Parlophone label.

This is terrific news! And the many people who voted The Beatles the No. 1 Rock 'n' Roll group on Merseyside will now have the opportunity to vote again for their favourite beat music entertainers—this time by voting their first disc a hit, and by buying copies as soon as it is released in July. At this stage, we regret we cannot reveal the titles of the disc, but further information will be given in our next issue.

Now here's where our readers can help us! We at Mersey Beat have often wondered which two songs, suitable for a single disc, our readers would most like The Beatles to record. There are so many numbers that this dynamic group does so well that we do not pretend the task will be an easy one. But please let us know what you think. Write in immediately giving reasons for your choice. We shall publish the results and award a prize to the writer of the best letter received, in the opinion of the Editor. Send your letters to this address: Mersey Beat, 81a Renshaw Street, Liverpool 1. The closing date will be next Wednesday, June 6th—so please hurry. We shall look forward to reading your letters.

Guitar Corner
by Bob Hobbs & Hu Biroh

THE BLACK BISON
(Available at Rushworth & Dreaper)

This much-awaited new model has four pick-ups with two rotary switches allowing eight permutations in pre-set tone colours. The pick-up arrangement and wiring is designed to give a new system of Split-Sound. The bass frequencies on pick-up can be eliminated from the treble which can then be auto-coupled to the bass on pick-up three. It has specially designed tremolo arm plus bridge unit and fitted in the heel of the neck is a precision "Gear Box" which is coupled to the steel truss rod in the neck and gives micromatic adjustment of the neck pitch.

The machine heads are completely enclosed, even the string barrels have a cover. Again, all metal parts are gold plated. Price: £157 10s. 0d.

MERSEY BEAT EXCLUSIVE STORY

BEATLES CHANGE DRUMMER !

Ringo Starr (former drummer with **Rory Storm and the Hurricanes**) has joined **The Beatles**, replacing **Pete Best** on drums. Ringo has admired The Beatles for years and is delighted with his new engagement. Naturally he is tremendously excited about the future.

The Beatles will fly to London to make recordings at E.M.I. Studios. They will be recording numbers that have been specially written for the group, which they have received from their recording manager **George Martin** (Parlophone).

THE BEATLES TO PLAY CHESTER

As a result of the phenominal Box Office success of The Beatles during their 4-week season of Monday nights at the Plaza Ballroom, St. Helens, the directors of Whetstone Entertainments, controllers of the ballroom, have engaged The Beatles for a series of four Thursday night sessions at the Riverpark Ballroom, Chester, which commenced on 16th August.

PETE BEST

Courtesy of Bill Harry/Merseybeat Archive

Yes I'm Gonna Be A Star...

The sacking of Pete Best in favour of Ringo Starr in the August of 1962 was as important a change for the image of the Beatles as it was a musical one. Although producer George Martin has since made it clear that the crucial motive for Best's replacement *was* musical, and instigated by himself – he didn't think the drummer was good enough for the recording studio – many of the underlying dissatisfactions with Best are thought to have been linked with the group's image.

In the mould of the American pop stars popular at the time, smooth clean heroes like Fabian and Bobby Vee, Pete was considered the "good looking" one of the Beatles. He certainly looked the most conventional, the least odd of the four. Rumours surrounding his dismissal claimed that the others were jealous of his particular popularity with the Liverpool fans, and that he refused to "mop top" his hair; whatever the cause, there was clearly some dissatisfaction with Pete's image in the group on the part of John, George and Paul – and possibly Brian Epstein – which was brought to a head with Martin's more fundamental criticisms.

Ringo was a fortunate choice, the last piece in the jigsaw. His hang-dog expression was suitably individual and, like the others, he didn't look like the pop stars of 1962; with them, he was to become one of *the* pop stars of 1963.

It was immediately after Ringo's entry into the group that photographer Dezo Hoffmann got involved with the Beatles. Indeed, his 1962 shots in Abbey Road studios all featured George Harrison with his right profile to the camera, to disguise the black eye he received from an irate Pete Best fan on the announcement of the former drummer's departure.

Dezo Hoffmann first photographed the Beatles as a staff photographer for the *Record Mirror*. They were local heroes in Liverpool but still meant little elsewhere; a fan had written to the paper complaining of the music press's ignorance of the group, so Hoffmann was sent to cover them. So began a four-year working relationship in which

Hoffmann became the semi-official "court photographer" of the Beatles.

Born in Czechoslovakia, Hoffmann began work as a clapper boy in a Prague film studio before moving to Paris in the mid-'30s. From there he was sent to cover Mussolini's invasion of Abyssinia, the "alternative" to Hitler's 1936 Olympics held in Barcelona, and eventually the Spanish Civil War. It was in Spain that he worked alongside the likes of Robert Capa and Ernest Hemingway as part of the International Brigade Press Corps.

He arrived in England during the Second World War, after which he moved away from news photography to specialise as a freelance in the

Dezo Hoffmann: The Beatles under blue suburban skies, in Paul's back garden.

entertainment field. Concentrating on such celebrity subjects as Marilyn Monroe, Charlie Chaplin and Louis Armstrong, Hoffmann joined the staff of *Record Mirror* in 1955. It was this that led to his eventual involvement with the Beatles.

Hoffmann's earliest sessions with the group, particularly those in Liverpool, marked a move away from the urban landscapes and "bomb site" realism of Les Chadwick's settings to the more rural environments of Paul McCartney's back garden and Liverpool's Sefton Park – a move Hoffmann recalls as a deliberate attempt to clean up their image still further. Ironically, it was out of the Sefton Park sessions that there came the famous "leaping in the air" shot used in mid-1963 as the cover for the *Twist and Shout* EP – where it was superimposed on a "bomb site" background.

The photographs sum up the Beatles' appearance at the time, having moved completely away from their former "rocker" look, with gingham shirts, polo-neck sweaters, suede "Chelsea boots" and short jackets – a look pinpointed in one of a series of articles in the London *Evening Standard* by Maureen Cleave, which the Beatles disclaimed because they felt it made them sound "queer".

The photographs, the spots on the radio and the touring package shows were all increasing, and in February 1963 the real breakthrough came – their second single *Please Please Me* reached No. 1 in the national charts. The Beatles had arrived and, within weeks, their music – and their image – was to become a national obsession.

Dezo Hoffmann: Sefton Park.

Dezo Hoffmann: Backstage at the Liverpool Empire, the Beatles celebrate their fist No. 1. The photographer in the foreground is Mike McCartney.

Dezo Hoffmann: The famous jump.

Please Please Me

I t was normal record company practise to put out a debut album *only* after a pop act had achieved a hit single, and to include that single as the main selling point of the album; and so it was with the Beatles. But the album, like all their albums to come, became an event in its own right. Their two singles, *Love Me Do* and *Please Please Me*, plus their respective B sides, were dutifully included, but in many ways it was the other tracks that established the identity of the album from the start.

Here, for the vast majority of listeners unfamiliar with the Beatles' club repertoire, was a cross section of their best – from the irresistable opening bars of *I Saw Her Standing There* to the climactic end on *Twist And Shout*: a perfect balance of originals and some of the best from the American pop writers of the period – the latter including Carol King's *Chains*, Arthur Alexander's *Anna* and Bacharach and David's wonderful *Baby Its You*.

As with the policy of including hit singles, the cover too followed record company convention; not only was the title that of the No.1 hit, but *Love Me Do* was also billed on the sleeve. Originally, the cover picture was to have been one by Dezo Hoffmann taken on the steps of Abbey Road studios, but the eventual choice was one from the now-famous stairwell session by Angus McBean – who, like Hoffmann was an established name in photography, specialising in theatrical and show business subjects. It was McBean who returned to the setting in 1969, on John Lennon's suggestion, for the *déja vu* session featured eventually on the *Beatles 1962-66* and *1967-70* compilations; the photograph was originally intended for the *Get Back* album of 1969, which eventually became *Let It Be* with a cover more directly related to the film.

The image on *Please Please Me* became one of a series of national symbols of the Beatles through 1963, when the album stayed at the No.1 LP chart position for an incredible 30 weeks from its release in March – until it was replaced at the top by *With The Beatles* – staying in the top ten albums for a total of 62 weeks.

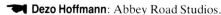 **Dezo Hoffmann**: Abbey Road Studios.

Dezo Hoffmann: The famous low bow.

Dezo Hoffmann: On the beach at Weston-super-Mare, taken on the summer tour of 1963.

Yeah, Yeah, Yeah

The Beatles spent much of 1963 touring in Europe and the UK – first as support to other, often American, stars then very quickly after March as invariable bill-toppers. As the welter of publicity increased, the Beatles own stage act provided the strongest base for the development of their public image, as well as for the press's perception of it. A case in point was their performance of their third single, *From Me To You*, which had the catchy "whoo" linking the chorus and the verse; at this point on stage, George, Paul and John would shake their heads in unison, and the gesture soon became part and parcel of the "mop top" persona.

Other onstage visual trademarks included the low bow with which they closed their act, the static poses they adopted during performance (as opposed to Shadows-like dance routines) which established a strong visual unity, and the fans' showering of the group with jelly babies after George had inadvertently mentioned the sweets in an interview.

Altogether, their style was getting more cuddly, more acceptable to all the family. Two memorable Dezo Hoffmann photo' sessions reflected this. The "on the beach" pictures taken at Weston-super-Mare while on a tour of seaside resorts had the boys in joke Edwardian bathing costumes and straw boaters – very English, very music hall, and very much family fun.

The studio sessions with Hoffmann established what was to become the most marketed image of the Beatles, in the grey collarless suits by Pierre Cardin, chosen at the advice of Brian Epstein. This was the image of the summer of '63, of *She Loves You*, of "Yeah Yeah Yeah" and of Beatlemania.

She Loves You, while continuing the falsetto "whoos" of *From Me To You*, included an even more potent gimmick, the "Yeah, Yeah, Yeah" which was perfect for the press coverage of the increasingly frantic tours – a press coverage that, by the autumn of 1963, had coined the word Beatlemania.

October 13th 1963 was the day when the word

Dezo Hoffmann: The new studio image. ☛

was born – on page one of all the popular daily papers after a particularly riotous appearance at the London Palladium. The subsequent Royal Command Performance a few weeks later set the seal on their acceptance as national idols, their image as utterly cute and harmless.....and fun, as evidenced by this *Daily Mirror* editorial the following day:

"YEAH, YEAH, YEAH"

You have to be a real sour square not to love the nutty, noisy, happy handsome Beatles. If they don't sweep your blues away, brother you're a lost cause. If they don't put a beat in your feet, sister you're not living. How refreshing to see these rumbustious young Beatles take a middle-aged Royal Variety Performance by the scruff of their necks and have them beatling like teenagers....The Beatles are whacky. They wear their hair like a mop, but it's WASHED, it's super-clean. So is their fresh young act....

The summer of '63 also saw for the first time – with the grey collarless suits as prime logo – the upsurge of Beatles merchandising. There was nothing new in merchandising, of course; since the pre-war years Mickey Mouse, Donald Duck, then Superman and even Davy Crockett, had appeared on clothes and other goods around the world. But most of this was American-based, and almost all aimed at a pre-'teen children's market. In Britain, in addition to American imprints, there were local comic book heroes like Dan Dare and television characters such as Muffin the Mule and Sooty – again strictly kid's stuff.

The only marketing of this kind to feature a pop star on a large scale, aimed at teenagers rather than (or as well as) children, was American, with the plethora of Elvis Presley material in the late '50s. For a British pop act to exploit their image in this way was unprecedented.

The Beatles appeared everywhere; cosmetics, toys, bubble gum, bed clothes, wallpaper, and an avalanche of (mostly unofficial) printed material, "souvenir" books and pictures.

In addition, there appeared numerous advertisements for Beatle-style clothing – cuban-heeled boots, collarless jackets – often spelled "Beetle style" to avoid infringements of copyright. The Beatles' choice of clothes to a large extent dictated teenage fashion for the following months, by which time the group themselves were anticipating the next trend; and by their grip on the nations' consciousness through the media, merchandising and advertising, moulding those trends.

It was during their seaside resorts tour of 1963 – at Bournemouth – that the Beatles were first photographed by Robert Freeman. One of a new breed of young photographers, his stark black-and-white compositions appealed to the Beatles sense of style, and he became very quickly a regular member of their (by necessity increasingly private) circle. In fact, when the Beatles separated from their initially communal London accomodation, it was Freeman and his wife who found a flat for John and Cynthia Lennon at their own address at Emperor's Gate off the Cromwell Road. Much of Freeman's work in late '63 and throughout 1964 exemplified the "grainy" style of photography synonymous with the mid-'60s, a style already apparent in the work of journalistic and "art" photographers, but a breakthrough in pop photography - and a breakthrough on a million-selling scale when Freeman's photography was used for their second album, *With The Beatles*.

With The Beatles

Where the cover of *Please Please Me* reflected the pop record conventions of the previous few years, *With The Beatles* abolished them once and for all. Instead of garish colour and B-movie typography, the title was plainly set, small, above the four side-lit black and white Beatles. A grainy texture, almost pointilliste in effect, gave the unsmiling fab four an unreal look, the mop tops suggestive of the dread Beatle wigs about to materialise on the American side of the Atlantic; black polo-neck sweaters achieved total isolation of the faces on the black background. This was not the "nutty, noisy, happy Beatles" beloved of the *Daily Mirror*. While the record sold in its hundreds of thousands (and eventually millions) to the growing legions of devotees – *everyone* now seemed to buy the Beatles' records – the cover clearly wanted them to be taken seriously; they were here to stay.

The balance of music was similar to that of their debut LP, with American rhythm-and-blues classics (early Motown, Chuck Berry, Smokey Robinson), a Broadway musical song (*'Till There Was You* from *The Music Man*) and originals, but there were hints of growing maturity in the latter; *All My Loving*, in particular, was the first song by Lennon and McCartney to be covered extensively by other artists – an early "standard" on their part.

By early 1964, when *With The Beatles* had been available for only a couple of months, the cover had become, and has remained, one of the most familiar – if not *the* most familiar – images in Beatles iconography. The picture has been used over the years, unofficially as often as not, on hundreds of items, from posters and books to mugs and t-shirts. If there has been one album cover which represents a key aspect of the Beatles' image, then *With The Beatles* – which, in the US, as their debut album was called *Meet The Beatles* – is that album.

I've Just Seen A Face

While the Beatles became a household name throughout the UK, the medium of their visual impact was still primarily the photograph (and, of course, their "live" image, either on stage or on television). Significantly, the first painters to feature them in their work were both Liverpool artists, Adrian Henri and Sam Walsh, whose styles reflected different streams in the pop art movement.

Pop art had developed as a genre, both in Britain and the United States, through the middle and late '50s. One of its major elements was the incorporation into "art" of the "non-art" of everyday commercial advertising and design – Coca Cola signs, chrome-bumpered cars, pintables and billboards – but almost invariably (with British painters as well as American) the subject matter was American. Like pop music in the '50s, pop art turned to America for inspiration, seeing in it the source of all that was new in terms of subject matter and imagery. British pop artists like Richard Hamilton and Peter Phillips rarely dealt with "English" imagery; only Peter Blake made parochialism a virtue in his work.

Pop art also sought to identify itself with, and perhaps justify, other forms of pop (in its real sense of "popular") culture – for example pop music, comic books and advertising. Pop artists defined their work as instant, accessible, even disposable. Richard Hamilton's definition of the essence of pop ran: "popular, transient, expendable, low cost, mass-produced, young, witty, sexy, gimmicky, glamorous, and last, but not least, Big Business". All this was fine in theory, but in practise – compared to pop music at least – pop art was defeated by its own internal contradictions; it could not be genuinely innovative; it was condemned to follow rather than to lead.

When Andy Warhol painted his Cambells Soup cans in the early '60s, they may have looked very contemporary – very *instant* – compared to the traditional subjects of the artist. But the design itself had been around for a generation. Like the Coca Cola logo, it was chosen *because* of a familiarity already established on the billboard and magazine page over many years. Similarly, his major human subjects from the worlds of cinema

Andy Warhol: Screen-printed over four Dezo Hoffmann portraits, this first appeared as the cover for the Rolling Stones publication *The Beatles* in 1980.

Adrian Henri

Adrian Henri: "Entry of Christ into Liverpool"....before the Beatles – unfinished, c. 1962.

Adrian Henri

....with the Beatles – finished, 1963.

and rock'n'roll were Marilyn Monroe and Elvis Presley, both familiar images, and already of the past rather than the present. Significantly, it was not until 1980 that Warhol got around to the subject of the Beatles. Pop art managed to reflect "real"pop, but hardly to emulate it; it would always remain one step behind, rather than ahead of, the times.

Although painters in Liverpool were doubtless aware of the Beatles' existence during their days of purely local acclaim – and certainly knew of Sutcliffe and Lennon from their art school days – the musical tastes of the artistic bohemia of Liverpool 8 were largely aloof from the Merseyside beat scene until the Beatles began to emerge at a national level in 1963.

Adrian Henri, although influenced by the American pop artists – particularly Jasper Johns and Robert Rauschenberg – had always used "local" images (plastic daffodils among the Omo packets, dead birds in Liverpool 8) and had often

mixed them with characters from his personal mythology. It was this juxtaposition of friends and heroes against the background of Liverpool that culminated in the cinemascopic *Entry of Christ Into Liverpool* (a homage to James Ensor's *Entry of Christ Into Brussels*), completed in early 1964. Among poets, painters, musicians and others in Henri's Pantheon, stand the Beatles. They are not particularly prominent; in fact, you have to look hard to find them. The most noticeable figures are Jarry's Père Ubu and jazz musician Charlie Mingus. It is an interesting social document, apart from its merits as a painting, and it is significant that by 1963 (swiftly by pop art reaction standards) the Beatles had earned their place in the assembly.

Henri was becoming known as a poet, one of the founding fathers of the Liverpool poetry scene. The Beatles as figures of local, then national, mythology inevitably crop up in the works of Henri and his best-known contemporaries, Roger McGough and Brian Patten. As an illustration,

Cover of *The Liverpool Scene* featuring photographs of the Beatles by Philip Jones-Griffiths; the book that launched the Liverpool poets in 1967, originally published by Donald Carroll.

two examples from Henri:

"....At the inquest of Paul McCartney, aged 21, described as a popular singer and guitarist, WPC Smith said, in evidence, that she saw one of the accused, Miss Jones, standing waving bloodstained hands shouting "I got a bit of his liver" "

From the new *Our Times* (January 1964)

and from the same year, another of Henri's homages to his heroes:

If you weren't you, who would you like to be?
Paul McCartney Gustave Mahler
Alfred Jarry John Coltrane
Charlie Mingus Claude Debussy
Wordsworth Monet Bach and Blake

Charlie Parker Pierre Bonnard
Leonardo Bessie Smith
Fidel Castro Jackson Pollock
Ghandi Milton Munch and Berg

Bela Bartok Henri Rousseau
Rauschenberg and Jasper Johns
Lucas Cranach Shostakovitch
Kropotkin Ringo George and John

From *Me*, 1964

Although the Beatles were in no way involved in the Liverpool poetry scene, they were certainly aware of its existence; Paul McCartney's brother Mike became involved in the early "events" and "happenings" organised by Adrian Henri, as a prelude to his forming the Scaffold poetry-and-satire group with Roger McGough and John Gorman, and on at least one occasion Beatles in the persons of George and Ringo turned up to a poetry reading at the Hope Hall (now the Everyman Theatre) in Liverpool.

Sam Walsh, an Irish painter who had moved to Liverpool in the late '50s, cultivated a pop style in the early '60s modelled on the work of Larry Rivers and Francis Bacon, advertising and the cinema screen – culminating in enormous portraits that have the effect of close-ups in the movies. The oblique title to his portrait of Paul McCartney, *Mike's Brother*, also says something about the "local lads" feeling for the Beatles still prevalent in Liverpool in 1963; it was almost an attempt to preserve them in the circle of ordinary people. "It was Mike I knew, not Paul" explains Walsh.

Sam Walsh: Mike's Brother. ☛

Andre Deutsch

Sam Walsh/James Cassles

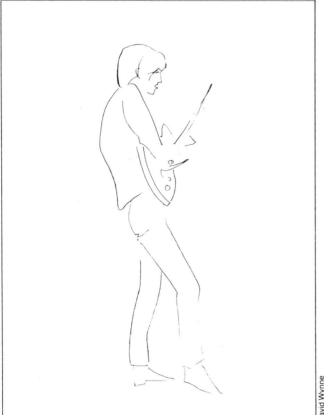

David Wynne

David Wynne: Sketch

David Wynne

David Wynne: Four figures.

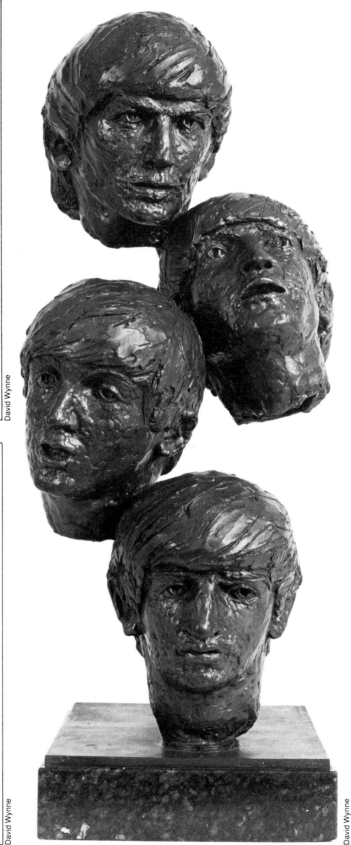

David Wynne

David Wynne: Four heads.

Flying

By early 1964, the Beatles had assumed the status of national figures, to the applause of Royalty, the press and the people. So when they sat, for the first and only time in their career, for a sculptor, it was for David Wynne, already known for his work with such prestigious names as Yehudi Menuhin and Sir Thomas Beecham. The session with Wynne produced four bronze heads and four small figures of the group. Wynne, whose later pieces have included the Prince of Wales and the EEC commemorative 50 pence piece, has stayed in touch with the former Beatles, particularly George, who recently gave him a ton block of

marble as a birthday present. The 1964 session with David Wynne, which took place in Paris while the group were playing a week's season at the Olympia concert hall, has another significance; it was the last artistic tribute to them as a purely British – or at least European – phenomenon. Within weeks, they were making their first trip to America.

The taking of America by the Beatles has been well documented, but their impact was not just due to their music. Much of it was to do with the way their image was exploited, in the press, advertising, television and – very quickly – merchandising. In a country as big as America, as

David Wynne: One of Wynne's own photographs of the Paris sculpture session.

THE BEATLES

the BEATLES ARE HERE!

London policemen fought to hold back 1,000 screaming teenagers when the Beatles made their getaway after a performance at the famous London Palladium. A motorcycle escort stood by as the four young singers rushed for their car. Then the fans went wild breaking through a blockade of more than 100 bobbies. They ran for the car missing it by seconds as it sped away.

It was the end of an unforgettable day-long seige at the Palladium. During rehearsals for the evening show, fifty girls managed to break through the doors, flood the stage and swarm around their idols until police cleared the hall.

The Beatles arrived in America in February after the over-whelming success of their "I Want To Hold Your Hand" single, which had pre-release orders of one million copies in England. They appeared on the Ed Sullivan Show, live from New York City and a second time from Miami Beach. A third appearance is scheduled during the season.

The impact of the Beatles on America has to do with their highly individual sound. It has been compared to a combination of Bo Diddley and The Dovells and emphasizes a group sound rather than a single guitar line. The solid rhythm and voicing has been dubbed the "Liverpool sound."

Who are these four gentlemen that caused mass hysteria in England and half of the free world?

TV-orientated as America, the only possibility for an unknown and foreign group to have any major impact was through the media. The Beatles' publicity assault on the American public has been described as the biggest media hype in show business history – and it worked. Not even Brian Epstein or Capitol Records (their US outlet), and certainly not the Beatles themselves, could have anticipated the extent of their immediate popularity in the States.

Their image – the suits, the boots, the accents and, most particularly the hair – was bizarre by American standards in a way it had never been in Britain. The suits were "cute", the accents "quaint" and the hair – well, like *long*. Hence the mop top side of their image was greatly exaggerated in America – in fact, it was in the United States that the ludicrous Beatles wigs first made their appearance.

Merchandising went wild, reaching levels unprecedented even during the height of Presley's popularity a few years before. Uniquely American items – and there were literally hundreds – included a "kiss your favourite Beatles" poster (with life size lips), a Beatles costume complete with mask, a long-eating liquorice record and a "Flip Your Wig" Beatles board game.

The details of how the Beatles themselves realised little of the merchandising royalties are complex and, to this day, not entirely clear, but nearly all items carrying an "official" logo utilized pictures by Dezo Hoffmann, or crude drawings based on his photographs. In the middle of 1984, Hoffmann was still compiling a marathon catalogue of everything that bore his pictures.

Over-the-top merchandising and hype notwithstanding, the Beatles' image in the States soon became identical to their image in England, particularly as record releases became simultaneous. (The first few months of American Beatlemania involved a lot of "catching up" by the US record company, hence at one point the Beatles occupied all the top five places in the US charts!) This "universal" image – for the rest of the world was swiftly falling under the Beatles' spell – took firmer shape in July 1964 with the release of their first feature film, *A Hard Day's Night*.

A Hard Day's Night

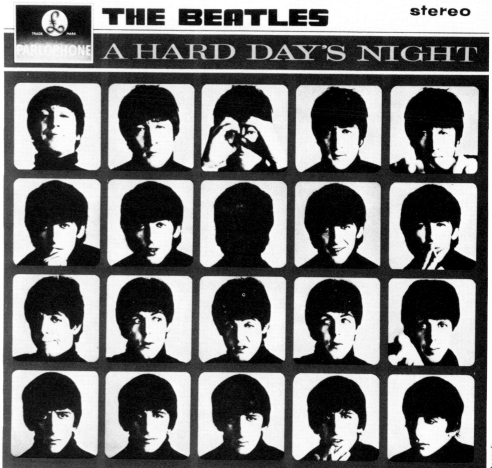

EMI Records

Unlike previous films concerned with pop music, the Beatles' debut feature film wasn't a *view* of pop from the (usually older) outside looking in, but *was* pop in itself. The only really enduring film to have come out of rock'n'roll had been Frank Tashlin's *The Girl Can't Help It*, and that was as a satire on the payola-stained realities of the US music business circa 1956. The rest had tended to be low budget excuses for a series of cameos, where Bill Haley, Little Richard, and other founders of rock, churned out their latest singles. Only Elvis embarked on a film career of any potential substance, and that melted after three or four films into a goo of celluloid marshmallow from which he was never truly to escape.

British rock fared no better in the cinema; *The Tommy Steele Story* was the nearest thing to biography, the rest were coffee-bar-and-youth-club epics even weaker (certainly on the musical side) than their American counterparts. Like Elvis, Cliff Richard took part in a couple of interesting items – *Express Bongo* and the little known *Serious Charge* – but none of this added up to much in terms of genuine pop cinema.

Like George Martin, Dick Lester, the director of *Hard Day's Night*, had a track record going back to the roots of British surrealist humour, with the much revered Goons; a fact that immediately qualified him in Lennon's eyes. He had worked with them on a zany short called *The Running, Jumping and Standing Still Film* in the late '50s, and a TV series along similar lines, *Idiots Weekly*. Both owed much to surrealism proper, and *Running, Jumping and Standing Still..* has become something of a cult classic.

Lester's first feature film was a fairly conventional pop vehicle, *It's Trad Dad* in which the "cameo" format was applied to the current (1961) fad for bowler-hatted traditional jazz bands and various non-jazz stars including Helen Shapiro.

A Hard Day's Night was a perfect chance for Lester to develop the visual ideas he had pioneered with the Goons; the script by Liverpool-based playwright Alun Owen was loose enough, the plot flexible enough, for him and the Beatles to improvise and develop ideas as they went along.

The speeded-up action, "silent movie" captions, the famous "running and jumping" sequence on the playing field – all established a Lester style that was to continue through *Help* and, later, *The Knack*. More importantly for the Beatles, it confirmed the image that they had built up over the past eighteen months; from the "leap in the air" pictures of Dezo Hoffmann in Liverpool and the grainy black-and-white portraits of Robert Freeman to the bouncy "mop tops" of stage and television appearances – all were reflected in, in fact reinforced by, the film. *A Hard Day's Night* simply *was* the Beatles.

The publicity graphics, which also formed the basis for the album cover, featured the "film strip" photographs of Robert Freeman and managed simultaneously to capture the feel of Dick Lester's direction in the film itself while continuing the side-lit image of the Beatles established by the *With The Beatles* album. The "strip" element made for great flexibility of use; the square album cover, rectangular movie-house posters, even a single strip running down the sides of London buses, all contained the same visual information at a glance – the Beatles. The poster for the Italian release of the film went so far as to make the "film strip" idea even more obvious by presenting the pictures as though they were an actual strip of film.

Musically, the album was another milestone. It was the first that had appeared to date with nothing but original compositions by Lennon and McCartney. Like the film, it just *was* the Beatles.

Poster for the Italian release of *A Hard Day's Night*.

Dear Sir Or Madam, Will You Read My Book

Earlier in the year, Jonathan Cape had published the first book of John Lennon's writings and drawings, *In His Own Write*. To those familiar with his schoolboy *Daily Howl* lampoons, or his *Beatcomber* column in *Merseybeat* (named after the humorous *Beachcomber* column in the *Daily Express*), it came as no surprise. To the world at large, and to the "serious" critics in particular, it was a revelation.

Some of the material was indeed from the *Daily Howl* period, returned in bulk by Rod Murray, who had "inherited" it when Lennon moved out of his Gambier Terrace flat to go to Hamburg. The book itself was a collection of Lennon's nonsense writing and surrealist visual wit – described by one critic as "Thurber-like drawings, Joycean prose and nonsense verse". The cover, designed and photographed by Robert Freeman, was applauded for its own elegance and originality when the book appeared.

On all sides, the Beatles were beginning to be associated with the newest and most relevant developments, not just in popular music, but in popular *style*.

With the books, the album covers, then the film graphics, Freeman was gradually assuming the crown of "court" photographer to the Beatles, which Dezo Hoffmann had worn since late 1962. Hoffmann's pictures were solid traditional photography, often geared to the show business publicity shot, but also totally candid when taken in a "live" (as opposed to a studio) situation. Freeman's work was studied, posed, contrived in the best sense of the word; it could be said that Freeman's work was *consciously* art, Hoffmann's *naturally* art.

Late into 1964, the Beatles were moving towards the consciously artful in various fields, though loudly eschewing the "bullshit" that went with it as they did so. At the same time, Freeman confirmed his position in the Beatle's inner circle when, in late November, *Beatles For Sale* was released.

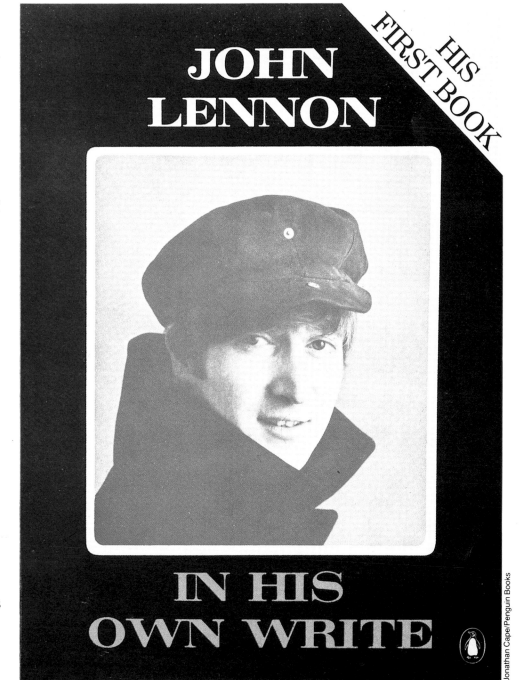

Robert Freeman: Cover for Lennon's *In His Own Write*.

Beatles For Sale

EMI Records

EMI Records

BEATLES FOR SALE

PMC 1240

This is the fourth by the four. 'Please Please Me', 'With The Beatles', 'Hard Day's Night'. That's three. Now. (1.), 'Beatles For Sale'.

The young men themselves aren't for sale. Money, noisy though it is, doesn't talk that loud. But you can buy this album—you probably have, unless you're just browsing, in which case don't leave any dirty thumbprints on the sleeve!

It isn't all currency or current though. There's priceless history between these covers. None of us is getting any younger. When, in a generation or so, a radio-active, cigar-smoking child, picnicking on Saturn, asks you what the Beatle affair was all about—'Did you actually know them?'—don't try to explain all about the long hair and the screams! Just play the child a few tracks from this album and he'll probably understand what it was all about. The kids of AD 2000 will draw from the music much the same sense of well being and warmth as we do today.

For the magic of the Beatles is, I suspect, timeless and ageless. It has broken all frontiers and barriers. It has cut through differences of race, age and class. It is adored by the world.

This album has some lovely samples of Beatle music. It has, for instance, eight new titles wrought by the incomparable John Lennon and Paul McCartney, and, mingling with the new, there are six numbers culled from the rhythmic wealth of the past extraordinary decade; pieces like Kansas City, and Rock and Roll Music. Marvellous.

Many hours and hard day's nights of devoted industry went into the production of this album. It isn't a potboiling quick-sale any-old-thing-will-do-for-Christmas mixture.

At least three of the Lennon-McCartney songs were seriously considered as single releases until John popped up with I Feel Fine. These three were Eight Days A Week, No Reply and I'm A Loser. Each would have topped the charts, but as it is they are an adornment to this LP, and a lesson to other artists. As on other albums, the Beatles have tossed in far more value than the market usually demands.

There are few gimmicks or recording tricks, though for effect, the Beatles and their recording manager George Martin, have slipped in some novelties. Like Paul on Hammond organ to introduce drama into Mr. Moonlight, which also, and for the first time, has George Harrison applying a thump to an elderly African drum because Ringo was busy elsewhere in the studio, playing bongos. George's thump remains on the track. The bongos were later dropped. Ringo plays timpani in Every Little Thing, and on the Rock and Roll Music track George Martin joins John and Paul on one piano. On Words Of Love, Ringo plays a packing case.

Beyond this, it is straightforward 1964 disc-making. Quite the best of its kind in the world. There is little or nothing on the album which cannot be reproduced on stage, which is, as students and critics of pop-music know, not always the case.

Here it is then. The best album yet—quite definitely, says John, Paul, George and Ringo—full of everything which made the four the biggest attraction the world has ever known. Full of raw John and melodic Paul; a number from George, and a bonus from Ringo. For those who like to know who does precisely what, there are details alongside each title.

DEREK TAYLOR

Side One (Lennon-McCartney)
1 NO REPLY (Lennon-McCartney)
Double tracked John. Occasionally Paul. George joins both on chorus.

2 I'M A LOSER (Lennon-McCartney)
Mainly John. Short passages by John and Paul.

3 BABY'S IN BLACK (Lennon-McCartney)
John and Paul

4 ROCK AND ROLL MUSIC (Berry)
John.

5 I'LL FOLLOW THE SUN (Lennon-McCartney)
Paul, double tracked here and there.

6 MR. MOONLIGHT (Johnson)
John.

7 KANSAS CITY (Lieber-Stoller)
Paul

Side Two
1 EIGHT DAYS A WEEK (Lennon-McCartney)
John and Paul. Occasionally George.

2 WORDS OF LOVE (Holly)
John and Paul

3 HONEY DON'T (Perkins)
Ringo sings.

4 EVERY LITTLE THING (Lennon-McCartney)
John and Paul.

5 I DON'T WANT TO SPOIL THE PARTY (Lennon-McCartney)
John and Paul.

6 WHAT YOU'RE DOING (Lennon-McCartney)
Paul.

7 EVERYBODY'S TRYING TO BE MY BABY (Perkins)
George sings.

Produced by GEORGE MARTIN   Photography by ROBERT FREEMAN   Recording first published 1964.

LONG PLAY 33⅓ R.P.M. • E.M.I. RECORDS LIMITED
(Controlled by Electric & Musical Industries Ltd.)
HAYES • MIDDLESEX • ENGLAND
Made and Printed in Great Britain

TRADE MARK OF THE PARLOPHONE Co., Ltd.

Use NEW EMITEX RECORD CLEANER

Ludwig THE BEATLES

uddenly the fringes were slightly out of control again; the mop top hair styles less certain, a sullen sureness peering through a dog-eyed worldliness among soft-focus woodlands. The back of the album sleeve conforms to what had become a '60s group-photo convention – "look up at the camera now lads, that's it…" – but the front, extra large woollen scarves prominent (a fashion within weeks), said it all. Despite the requirements of record sleeve tradition, even the "new" traditions they had established themselves over the previous year, the Beatles were their own men.

Inside (this was one of the earliest "gatefold" sleeves) were Freeman black-and-whites; a straight stage shot and an early homage/collage, predating *Sgt Pepper* by three years. It was Hollywood hero time, with Victor Mature, Jayne Mansfield and Ian Carmichael (not *just* Hollywood) among the stars of the silver screen. It was clear that the Beatles' past was not bounded by '50s rock'n'roll, or cover versions of it – appearing as it does almost for the last time on any of their albums.

As for their own songs, *Beatles For Sale* marked a move from "happy" pop songs to a more reflective stance – *I'm a loser, No Reply, Baby's In Black* – to which the front photograph (one of Freeman's relatively few colour sessions with the Beatles) provided a potent clue.

Robert Freeman: Collage.

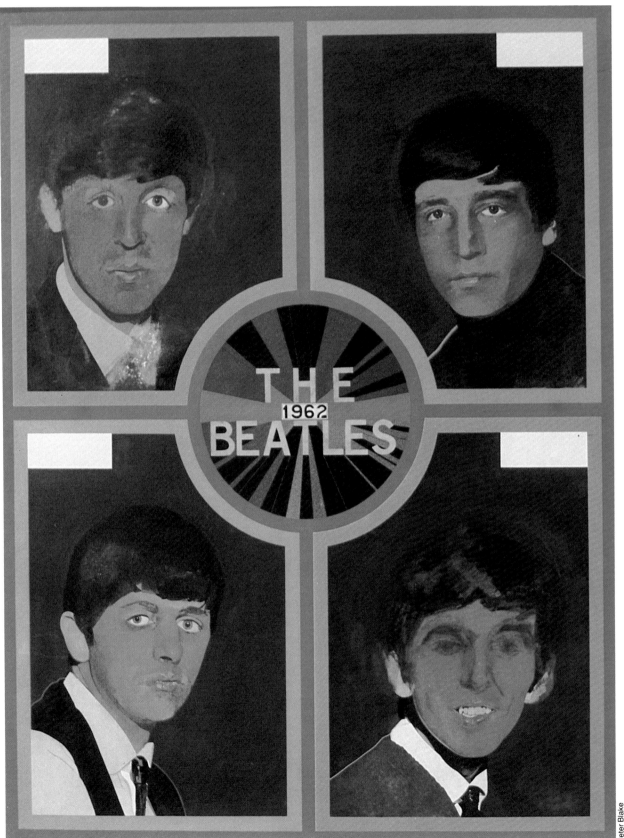

Peter Blake

Peter Blake: "Beatles 1962-67".

In his Pocket is a Portrait of the Queen

ntil a European tour in late June, all that most Beatle fans saw of the group in the first half of 1965 were occasional fleeting television appearances, including the *New Musical Express* poll winners concert at Wembley, when they appeared for the first time in military style jackets. Over the following year, the military look spread, until it became an indispensable feature of "swinging" London. It could, perhaps, be more accurately described as "mock military", a camped-up adaptation of Victorian and Edwardian regimental uniform jackets, all high collars, brass buttons and epaulettes. As befitted the "I'm backing Britain" era of Harold Wilson's administration, symbols of the country's imperial past – and the Union Jack in particular – were fashionable. During this phase of visual pop patriotism, period (or mock-period) graphics and posters, and shops like "I Was Lord Kitchener's Valet" added up to a new nostalgia – nostalgia for a caricature of the past rather than for the past itself – on the part of a youth generations away from the reality.

The "English" approach of Peter Blake's parochial pop art came into its own; the fairground barkers, the Fry's cocoa tins, the ephemera of bygone days decorated the pages of the style-setting glossies,*Town* and *Queen* magazines. The images of '50s America were discarded along with the art that went with them and, significantly,it was at this time that Blake began his large work "The Beatles 1962-67". And it was Blake whom the Beatles chose to orchestrate visually, two years later, the culmination of the nostalgic movement in the artwork for *Sgt Pepper's Lonely Hearts Club Band*.

The "1962" in the title, which appears under the Beatles' name in the picture, signifies the period from which Blake has drawn his image. Staring straight out of the camera, only George smiling, despite a certain "unfinished" quality, we instantly know who they are. There is no real need for the central logo save as part of Blake's labelling, which characterised much of his work in the middle '60s.

In fact, the caption was absent when the painting appeared on the cover illustration for the Penguin edition of George Melly's *Revolt into Style* in 1972.

John Lennon's second book was launched in June 1965 while the group were on a European tour – their first that year. *A Spaniard in the Works* was characterised by a more satirical slant than his first collection, which was basically straight nonsense, and the cover was again by Robert Freeman. Then, a month later, came another major event for the Beatles as a whole – the release of the single, album and feature film *Help*.

Jonathan Cape/Penguin Books

Poster for the Polish release of *Help*

Help

The new film, again directed by Richard Lester, was an altogether more extravagant venture. A parody of the James Bond type of thriller of the mid-'60s, *Help* avoided the semi-documentary style of *A Hard Day' Night* and involved the group in a fantasy adventure which set them in a variety of exotic locations, from Alpine ski slopes to the Bahamas.

Like the military look being adopted by the youth of England, the Beatles' style in *Help* was very much a case of "dressing up" – fashion was becoming fun and, in the film, the Beatles took this to an extreme that only a full-colour extravaganza could allow. Robert Freeman worked on the photography, and the soft-focus approach of *Beatles For Sale* permeated much of the film, particularly the scenes shot with the army on Salisbury Plain.

The main logo for *Help*, which formed the design for the album cover was the semaphore h-e-l-p, spelled out by all four Beatles, which became yet another of their trademarks, another of the symbols that were to make them instantly identifiable.

The music on the *Help* album included the songs from the film as the A side; strong yet melodic rock, the flavour of American folk-rock creeping in (especially in the Dylanesque *You've Got to Hide Your Love Away*) almost before the style had become firmly established in the United States itself; the chart-topping Byrds, who took the genre from Dylan to rock proper in the summer of 1965, admitted to having moved from folk to rock themselves the year before after seeing *A Hard Day's Night*.

The B side of the album included the final album tracks by the Beatles of others' material (*Act Naturally* and *Dizzy Miss Lizzy*) as well as the song that was to become the Lennon/McCartney "standard" *par excellence*, *Yesterday*: by the Beatles' standards, an "ordinary" album, simply a link between the previous and the following Christmas album releases; by the standards of the rest of rock, a classic of perfection.

EMI Records

Northern Songs

Robert Freeman

Robert Freeman: Ringo Starr in *Help*.

...Not So Self-assured

The release of *Help* heralded more frantic touring, making up for the previous six months spent in front of the film cameras. Beatlemania world-wide was at an absolute peak, and the Beatles' image was now so familiar and well established that – while they were on the road at least – it was, in a sense, taken out of the Beatles' control. Temporarily, they were powerless to change it.

Confirmation of this came with the showing in America of a TV cartoon series, made by the same London-based animation company who went on to create *Yellow Submarine*, TVC (TV Cartoons); the characters – and more especially the dubbed on American voices – were caricatures of the *popular conception* of the cuddly mop-tops, rather than caricatures of the Beatles as such. It was with the realisation that they were in danger of becoming caricatures *themselves*, in the constant claustrophobia of hotel rooms and fifty minute shows, that the Beatles finally asserted control of their image, grasping the reins firmly before the bandwaggon careered totally out of control.

Evidence to this effect came at the end of 1965, with the release of an album which hinted at traumatic developments in the Beatles' music – and image – to come.

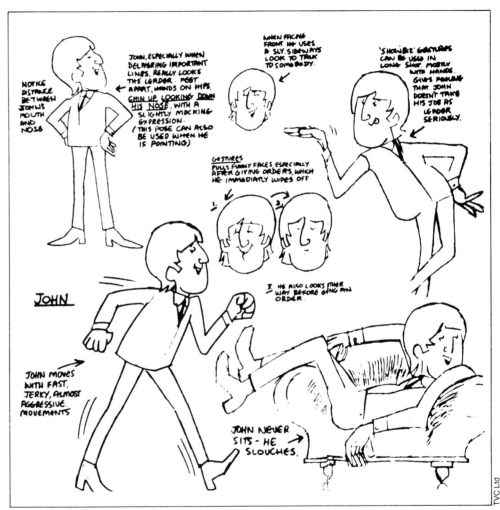

TVC: Annotated sketches.

Rubber Soul

Some members of the Beatles' fan club actually wrote complaining about the sleeve of *Rubber Soul*, saying it made their idols look like corpses. The distortion achieved by Robert Freeman, as if viewed reflected in water, certainly had a sinister edge to it; once again the Beatles were unsmiling, serious. Unusually for the time, their name was completely absent from the front cover – the image, albeit a disturbing one, was sufficient for instant and universal recognition.

As important as the photography on *Rubber Soul* was the typography, anticipating the earliest US-inspired psychedelia by nearly a year. The Disneyish lettering heralded a style that was to become the *de rigeur* of the poster art of the flower power sub-culture which blossomed on America's West Coast in 1966.

Musically, it was another landmark. The songs were more restrained, more accoustic, highly melodic and instantly memorable. There was innovation on every track – Lennon's surrealism emerging in *Norwegian Wood*, an increased introspection in *In My Life*; George growing in stature as a composer with *If I Needed Someone*, and introducing the sitar to rock on *Norwegian Wood*; Paul on fuzz bass on *Think For Yourself*, Ringo on Hammond organ in *I'm Looking Through You*.

Critics and fans alike agreed that the Beatles could develop no further; this surely was their peak. But they were wrong.

Rubber Soul was the final album to appear in what might be called the classic "middle period" of the Beatles, both as regards image and music. Their next release, *Revolver* in August 1966, coincided with the group's decision to give up touring, and marked a more self-consciously "artistic" (or "arty" as their few detractors would have it) stance. It was at this point that the explosion of the Art of the Beatles could truly be said to have begun.

EMI Records

It Could Make A Million For You Overnight.....

What distinguished the latter part of the '60s, as far as pop was concerned, was that it was becoming part of a whole sub-culture of youth rather than just the music of youth. Rock, as it was becoming known to its most fashionable afficionados, represented a whole lifestyle, not just an entertainment and leisure activity. And although music provided the nerve centre for this emerging counter culture, most of its secondary manifestations were visual – in clothes, graphics, illustration and even animation.

The sub-culture that emerged had its impetus, and many of its roots, in the United States rather than in England. This was a significant development: during the mid-'60s (after the "British invasion" of 1964) English style and fashion had led the way, with American youth always appearing to be at least two years behind the times. And when the British explosion became manifest on the other side of the Atlantic, the resulting visual styles were, in many ways, a parody of the real thing. The clothes that had evolved from the designs of Mary Quant and others – mini-skirts, "shift" dresses, see-through lace – along with often gross exaggerations of the paisley shirts and flamboyant trousers of Carnaby Street, became American "mod" style. Not until the youth "revolution" of the latter part of the decade did America resume its pre-Beatles position as the central influence on the consciousness of the world's youth, and even though Britain's cultural domination came to an end, recent history ensured that developments in England would always remain influential.

The Beatles, once again anticipating changes and in doing so helping bring them about, were central to these developments – both musically and visually their influence shaped the late '60s profoundly. The watershed period in these changes is generally considered to have been the summer of 1967, the summer of "flower power", the beautiful people and Sgt Pepper. But the real breakthrough started a year earlier.

Already influential artists and writers, and very soon the Beatles, the Beach Boys, the Rolling Stones and Bob Dylan (the taste-makers of pop), were experimenting with the consciousness-expanding drug LSD. The drug, at the time, was still to be made illegal; it was tasteless, colourless and apparently harmless, in that it was non-addictive (evidence as to the damage it inflicted on brain cells was still to emerge). Its main propagandist was Dr Timothy Leary, an American psychologist, who "dropped out" into a full-time role as prime spokesman for the new drug culture. "Turn on, tune in, drop out" was his slogan to the generation of American teenagers faced with the contradictory realities of the '60s, the "high and low" extremes of rock and the Beatles, and the war

Dezo Hoffmann: John Lennon in hippy attire, 1967.

Tetsusaburo Shimoyama

in Vietnam. The properties of LSD were "visual" in that its most pronounced effect was on visual perception. Its use promoted, therefore, among lyricists and other writers, a more visual approach. Song writers – Lennon and McCartney among them – who had by and large written in "abstract" terms in the classic love song tradition, now began working on a broader canvas, full of potent observation and imagery.

An interesting curiosity, perhaps in some way a product of this increase in visual awareness, is the painting (said to be the only one of its kind) done by all four Beatles in a Tokyo hotel bedroom in 1966, at the request of the manager. Starting from each corner, the Beatles signed the work in the centre to indicate their respective handiwork. The abstract work – in which Ringo's contribution comes over as the most positive, certainly the most "hard edged" – is the closely guarded property of a Japanese collector, a former president of the Japanese Beatles Fan Club (an institution with more members today than it had even in the mid-'60s), and the original has never been seen outside Japan.

Stylistically, the initially two-dimensional nostalgia of "Lord Kitchener's Valet" and Union Jack mugs had led the way to a fashion for the Art Nouveau of the early century, and the work of illustrators in particular, notably Alphonse Mucha and Aubrey Beardsley. Although there was a parallel vogue for the Victorian Pre-Raphaelite painters, it is significant that it was the illustrators whose work enjoyed the biggest revival, no doubt because of its easy application to the modern environment of postcards, book illustration and the growing industry of the decorative poster. During the summer of 1966 an exhibition of Beardsley's work at London's Victoria and Albert Museum drew unprecedented crowds, most of them young; this for an artist most of their grandmothers would have called "old fashioned". Beardsley's hallucinogenic associations and dabblings in erotica set him apart from many of his contemporaries of course, but in style he was part of the mainstream of Art Nouveau illustrators.

Lennon, Harrison, McCartney and Starr: The legendary "hotel" painting by all four Beatles.

Revolver

Robert Freeman

Robert Freeman: John Lennon, 1966, used by Klaus Voorman in the *Revolver* collage.

Within weeks of the Beardsley exhibition, the new album by the Beatles, *Revolver*, appeared, with a cover by their old friend from the art school crowd in Hamburg, Klaus Voorman. Again the Beatles' name did not need to appear; just "Revolver" in simple bold lettering, below a collage of tiny photographs of the group peeping through four thin line drawings of their faces, clearly inspired by Beardsley's style and reflecting the current popularity of that style. The back cover photograph, by Robert Whittaker, included Ringo in wire-framed "granny" style sunglasses, John in "Mr Pickwick" glasses and Paisley shirt – all indicative of the fashion of the times.

The music reached new heights of importance in the visual quality brought to the Beatle's recordings in Revolver. *Eleanor Rigby*, full of surreal images side by side with a sad reality ("all the lonely people"); the ultimate '60s children's rhyme, *Yellow Submarine*, inspiration for a film-full of characters with sound-effects that were truly visual in themselves; and the maturing of Lennon's surrealist lyrics, disturbing images from inside rather than outside his head ("listen to the colour of your dreams") in *Tomorrow Never Knows*.

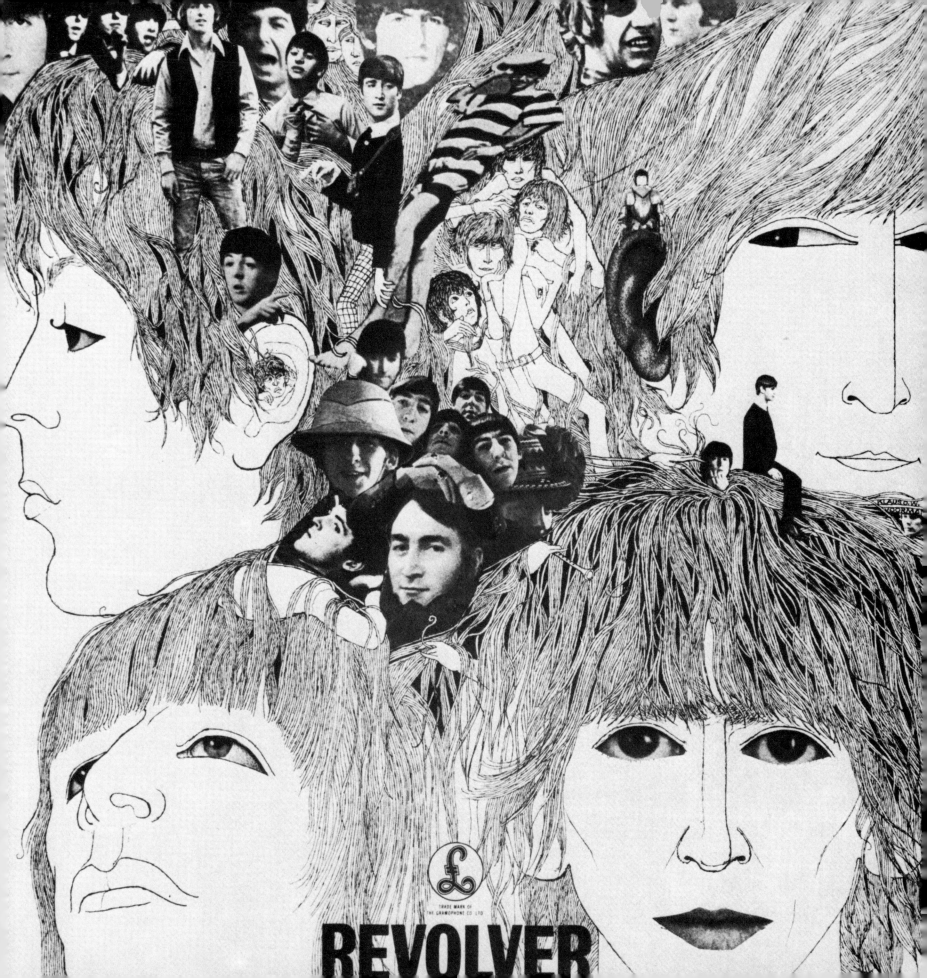

In My Ears And In My Eyes

Revolver also provided some Beatle subject matter for a young artist Alan Aldridge, whose work was to become archetypal of pop-inpsired illustration in the late '60s, when he produced "life masks" of Paul and Ringo as Eleanor Rigby and the Yellow Submarine respectively. At the time Art Director for Penguin Books, Aldridge became further involved in rock illustration with his cover for the Who's *A Quick One* in 1967. He had already designed the cover for the Penguin edition of John Lennon's two books,

featuring photographs by Duffy.

Drawing on images far wider than than just those of Art Nouveau – Walt Disney, '30s British children's comics, '50s Americana – Aldridge utilized a technical brilliance based in commercial design to achieve an extravagant, exotic style. He went on to design and coordinate overall the ambitious *Illustrated Beatles* in which he and other prominent illustrators and photographers interpreted visually the Beatles' song lyrics. Aldridge's other major piece of Beatles design was

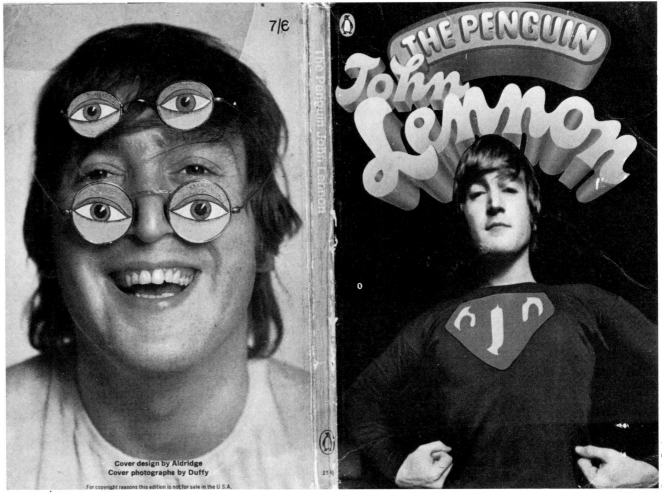

Cover design by Aldridge
Cover photographs by Duffy
For copyright reasons this edition is not for sale in the U.S.A.

Penguin Books

Alan Aldridge: *The Penguin John Lennon*, 1966, with a cover designed by Alan Aldridge incorporating photographs by Duffy.

the cover for the Hunter Davies authorised biography. Stylistically his work, while drawing from many sources as instanced above, reminded one of the richly festooned screens fashionable in Edwardian sitting rooms

With its flamboyant typography, surreal settings and explosions of colour, Aldridge's work between '66 and '69 became synonymous with psychedelia – a style which found its major musical totem in the Beatles masterpiece, released in the "flower power" summer of 1967, *Sgt Pepper's Lonely Hearts Club Band*.

"Pepper" was preceded by a long period of of seclusion on the part of the Beatles, a seclusion mainly in the recording studio. *Revolver* had appeared in August 1966, and the promised Christmas season album – now a regular event – never materialised. The fans had to put up with an EMI compilation *A Collection of Beatles Oldies*, with a cover which reflected once again the nostalgia theme, this time '20s clothes, cars and an ancient wind-up gramophone.

The first manifestation of the Beatles studio work over the previous months came early in 1967 with the release of what came to be regarded by many as the finest single, both sides considered, in the history of popular music. A daring judgement, but not entirely unreasonable. The accuracy of McCartney's observation, "recollected in tranquility" in *Penny Lane*, combined with the totally compelling impressionism of Lennon's childhood contradictions in *Strawberry Fields* indeed made for a powerful release. An interesting visual side-product of the release was that when the Beatles appeared on an early TV "promotional film" (pre-dating today's promotional videos) they had all grown moustaches while away from the public gaze. The moustaches completed the "military" look which was to find its final expression on the cover of *Sgt Pepper*, a cover which was to become the most celebrated in the history of the recording industry.

Alan Aldridge: "Cry Baby Cry", 1969, from the *Illustrated Beatles*.

Alan Aldridge: John Lennon, 1969, from the *Illustrated Beatles*.

Alan Aldridge: "All You Need Is Love", 1969, from the *Illustrated Beatles*.

Sgt Pepper's Lonely Hearts Club Band

Sgt Pepper has since been recognized as the pinnacle of the Beatles' achievement; not as innovative as *Revolver*, but bringing together all the strands of that album's innovation into one whole. It was the first "concept album", although in retrospect the link between the tracks is tenuous; the songs work perfectly well on their own. The Beatles' music was becoming increasingly "visual", the lyrics – as heralded in *Revolver* and *Penny Lane* – more directly literal and descriptive, creating a visual imagery around the Beatles over and above that which they presented in physical terms.

There were observations of contemporary life, in *Lovely Rita* and *She's Leaving Home* (another of the "lonely people"), a hint of nostalgia for childhood memories in *When I'm Sixty Four*. The revelations of hallucinogens on the other hand were vividly described at their most attractive (*Lucy In The Sky With Diamonds*) and terrifying (*A Day In The Life*). A more fairy-tale nostalgia, for the dissappearing (and dissappeared) world of the traditional music hall and circus, was exemplified in *Mr Kite* (taken from an actual poster, which apparently still hangs on the wall of Yoko Ono's New York apartment) and *Sgt Pepper* itself. And it was the nostalgic element, rather than the outright "psychedelic", which predominated on the Pepper sleeve. (Attempts at visually simulating the "acid trip" experience were invariably doomed to failure, hence a plethora of embarrassing late-'60s record covers, a trap the Beatles managed to avoid.)

The Sgt Pepper uniforms the Beatles themselves wore, were the military style of the previous year taken to its Ruritanian fairy tale extreme, like characters from a Sigmund Romberg operetta; but the setting they chose was what made "Pepper" a memorable visual event.

The Beatles' idea was to set a tableau of their various heroes and cultural mentors, with themselves as the "Pepper band" in the centre. No expense was spared, and to execute the task they engaged Peter Blake and his then wife Jann

Peter Blake

Peter Blake: Preliminary sketches for Sgt Pepper.

Haworth, who used nearly sixty life-size photographs as a montage against which stood the waxworks Sonny Liston, the Beatles c.1963, and the Beatles themselves. Arranged like an ornamental garden were the other manifestations of the Beatles' current preoccupations and past stimuli; an Indian goddess, a "Rolling Stones" doll, a portable television, a row of marijuana plants and "Beatles" spelt in flowers.

Centrepiece to the assemblage was the Sgt Pepper drumskin, which became in itself a part of the Beatles' iconography. Conceived by Blake and the Beatles, it was painted by a genuine fairground artist, Joe Ephgrave, who actually did two versions of what was to become the world's most famous drumskin.

After wrangles over the clearance of photographs (several had to be withdrawn eventually) the piece was set, and photographed for the cover by Michael Cooper. It became a popular game to try to identify all the faces – the list ranged from movie stars like Tom Mix and Marilyn Monroe and such visual artists as Aubrey Beardsley and Richard Lindner, to Lewis Carroll, Dylan Thomas and other writers. A list of the writers represented shows a marked emphasis on those who had themselves experimented with hallucinogens in pursuit of their art – Poe, Huxley and Burroughs for example; there was also an element of the English variety stage, with comedians Max Miller, Tommy Handley and Izzy Bonn, while philosophy was represented by Marx,

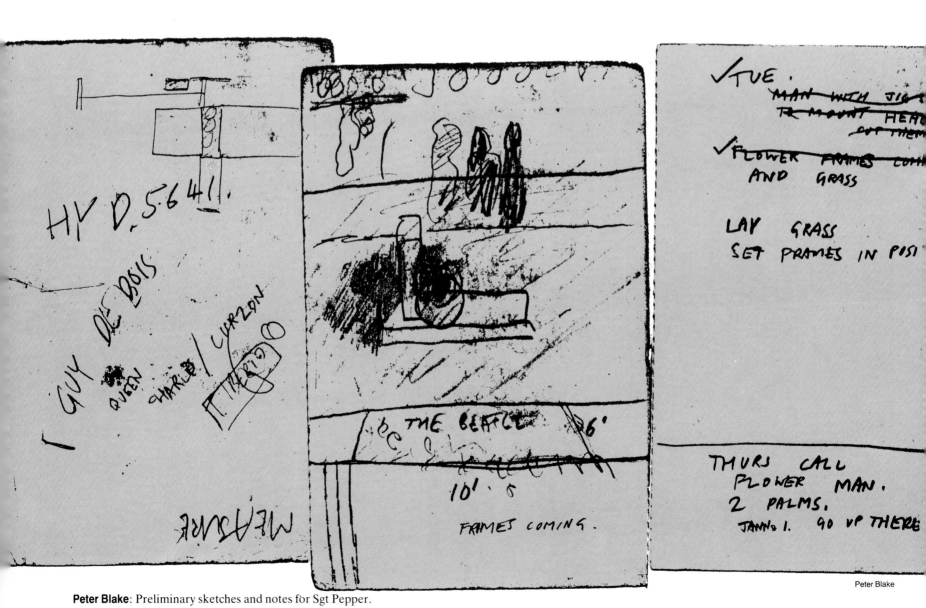

Peter Blake: Preliminary sketches and notes for Sgt Pepper.

Peter Blake

Paul McCartney

Joe Ephgrave: The alternative version of the Sgt Pepper drumskin.

Huxley and Jung. Surprisingly – but perhaps significantly – the only musicians present were pop singer Dion, Bob Dylan, Stuart Sutcliffe and the Beatles themselves.

Immediately following the photo' session, "souvenirs" from the tableau began to disappear, and little remains locatable today. Sonny Liston stands, arms folded, in Peter Blake's study; the Marlene Detrich cut-out belongs to a collector friend of Blake; Paul McCartney owns the "alternative" drumskin, the one used on the actual cover was photographed in John Lennon's Dakota Building flat a short time before his death.

Continuing the fun-nostalgia theme of Pepper ("A splendid time is guaranteed for all" concluded the back cover notes) an insert by

Blake and Haworth was included in the sleeve, featuring cut-outs of the good Sergeant's moustache, regimental stripes and so on – not that many owners of the record actually cut out the pieces, preferring rather to keep them as an integral part of the "event" – for that is what the cover concept of Sgt Pepper had become.

Sgt Pepper was indeed an event, from the music with its dubbed-on applause, to the sing-along lyrics on the back sleeve (unknown on pop albums until then), the cut-outs which few would cut out, and the all-embracing idolatry of the front cover. Rock music, and the art that increasingly accompanied it, would never be the same again.

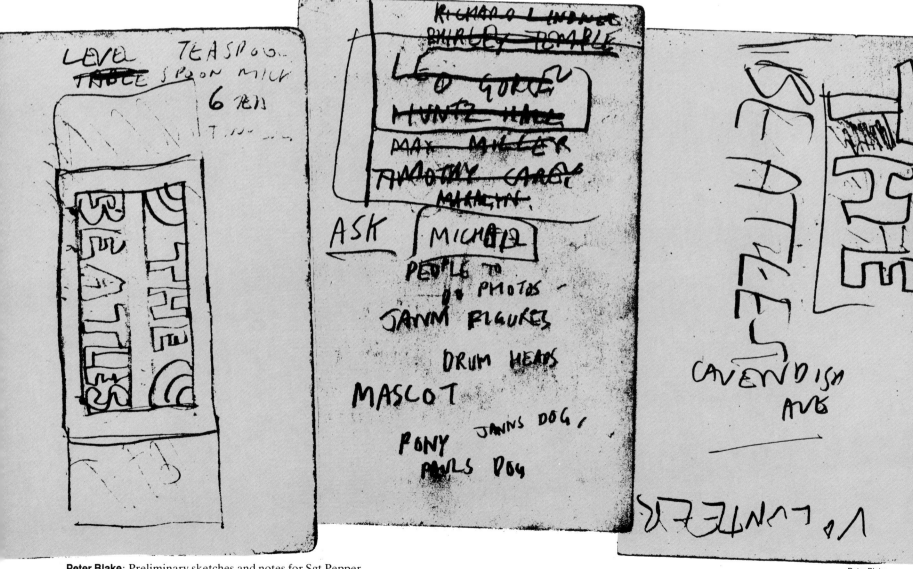

Peter Blake: Preliminary sketches and notes for Sgt Pepper.

Peter Blake

Sgt.Pepper

Peter Blake/**Jann Haworth**: Sgt Pepper insert.

John Bratby: Paul McCartney, 1967.

Love Is All You Need

The Beatles' patronage of Blake signified an increased interest in having their presentation (and consequently "image" in the broadest sense) associated with "real" artists, now they had assumed full control over these areas. Paul meanwhile became the subject rather than the creator when he sat for John Bratby for the only individual portrait of a Beatle since Sam Walsh's *Mike's Brother* back in 1963. Bratby was in many ways an "establishment" name; fashionable in the '50s (in fact an early influence on the figurative work of Stuart Sutcliffe), his style was considered *passé* against the sharp lines of pop and post-pop super-realism. But as always, McCartney was his own man – he sat for Bratby.

The summer of 1967 was the summer of love, and no sooner was Pepper released than the Beatles discarded their military fancy dress once and for all, in favour of the bells and beads of the hippy era. They publicly stated their commitment to the "love" ethos – and immediately became its prime acolytes, its high priests, when they appeared on the round-the-globe live TV broadcast "One World" on June 25th, on which they debuted *All You Need Is Love*. The song became the instant anthem for the flower people, and once again visual style was of the esence.

Although the "love" culture was, at its centre, an esoteric cult, based in hallucinogens and a philosophy largely alien to Western thought – dabbling in Eastern meditation and other exotic mysteries – it achieved, with the help of the Beatles, a remarkable degree of popularity. This popularisation was, of course, in many ways superficial. The Beatles themselves admitted to having taken LSD, but in general, the mass popularity of flower power didn't extend much beyond clothes and style. Inevitably, the whole thing got out of hand, with anodyne records like Scott MacKenzie's *San Francisco* ("…wear some flowers in your hair…") and the Flower Pot Men (!!) gracing the charts in the summer of 1967.

It could be argued that the Beatles function (sometimes unwittingly) as prime agents of popularisation, was to trivialise all they touched. However, they, more than any others, helped to broaden and therefore enrich, the catalogue of styles available to the mass consciousness during the '60s. It is the common paradox of popularisation that the marriage of sophisticated notions with popular taste dilutes the former while enriching the latter.

The most memorable graphic style to come directly out of the whole psychedelic period was the new genre of poster art – or more precisely, the West Coast school of poster art. The Disney-like lettering which had first appeared on *Rubber Soul* back in the winter of '65, had, through 1966, exploded on a thousand rock posters on America's West Coast, and by mid-'67 was established with the English "underground" culture too. Rendering

Dezo Hoffmann: The Beatles during the "One World" global TV broadcast in June 1967.

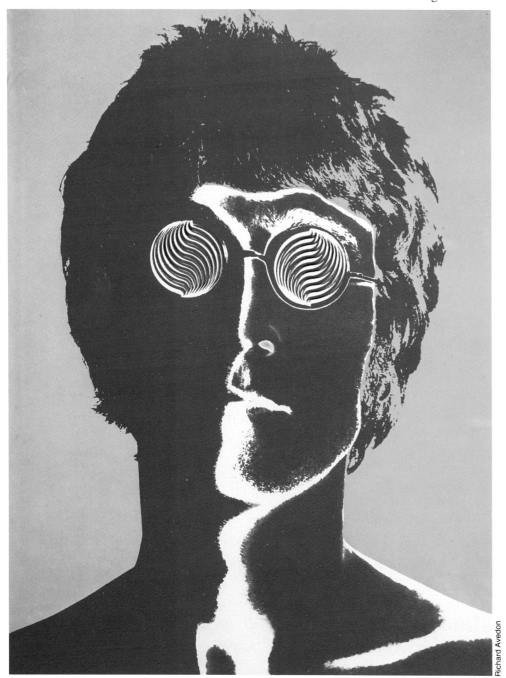

Richard Avedon

Richard Avedon: John Lennon 1968, one of the classic "psychedelic" posters.

lucrative medium for their work.

Best selling posters – there was even a poster "chart" for a time in one magazine – included propaganda themes, like the famous "Would you buy a used car from this man?" portrait of Richard Nixon and Alan Ginsberg as Uncle Sam, a variety of "legalise pot" designs, and straight challenges to good taste (Frank Zappa on the lavatory immediately springs to mind). There was also a boom in "old" posters – the Beardsley/Mucha fad continued – and "blow-up" portraits of vintage film stars, Theda Bara, Chaplin, Bogart and Monroe being among the most popular.

Posters featuring the Beatles proliferated in the 1970s, after the group had broken up, but the major work involving them in the late '60s was by American photographer Richard Avedon. His four "psychedelic" posters of 1968 have become classics of the genre; John with the "trippy" glasses, Ringo with the dove of peace – such images were made totally accessible by the mood of the times, to the extent that the posters were marketed in Britain through a special offer in the *Daily Express*!

A later poster published by Avedon was taken from a photograph he originally took for *Look* magazine in 1967. Interestingly, when EMI decided to use the picture on the cover and centrefold of the *Love Songs* compilation in 1977, they reversed Paul and Ringo's positions, the scale being altered accordingly.

In many ways posters could be said to obey the classic rules of pop which more traditional art – including pop art – could not; they were of their time, disposable, mass produced and cheap – all the things pop art had hoped to emulate, but couldn't.

The "underground" as such, the minority (albeit a large and growing minority) who embraced the alternative culture as lifestyle rather than mere fashion, also regarded the Beatles as its supreme spokesmen. Although the Beatles' involvement could be seen by cynics as at least only temporary if not downright opportunist, they managed, through their contribution to the music of the era and their sheer charisma, to transcend such considerations. Even among the cult-conscious young, the Beatles were able to bridge the gap between "pop" and "serious" attitudes, closing that gap in doing so; once again, they proved themselves the one *universal* figurehead of the times.

It is very easy to ridicule the whole psychedelic phase of course, particularly with hindsight, but at the time much of it seemed quite normal, just pop fashion taking another crazy turn as it was inclined

illegible much of the information they were supposed to convey, they were nevertheless highly decorative after the fashion of the times and so existed as "art" in their own right, their advertising function becoming secondary.

More important than that particular style however – which quickly dated as a fashion – was the establishment of the poster as such as art object. Photographers and illustrators on both sides of the Atlantic saw it as a valid and often

Gerald Scarfe

Gerald Scarfe: Fibreglass and *papier mâché* Beatles for the cover of *Time* magazine on September 22nd 1967.

to do in the '60s – and as usual, the Beatles were there ahead of the rest, anticipating, leading – then jumping off the bandwagon as it began to get too crowded, taking off in another direction altogether.

One visual commentator who did manage to sense a growing confusion in the Beatles' stance, however, was the cartoonist Gerald Scarfe. He had already drawn them during the time they were filming *Help*, but in 1967, *Time* magazine commissioned a cover featuring the group. Scarfe built four life-size models which were then photographed for the magazine, and produced a grotesque caricature that even his barbed pen and ink lines would have been inadequate to achieve – a long and winding road from the cuddly mop tops. The subsequent history of the *papier mâché* and fibreglass sculpture has its own irony; the flour

base to the *papier mâché* has had to be fumigated from time to time, after being attacked by biscuit beetles!

Magical Mystery Tour

EMI Records

It is generally conceded that the Beatles first venture after the death of Brian Epstein, the *Magical Mystery Tour* film, was also their first major artistic failure. Today, however, it comes over as a harmless romp through the fantasy world of the Beatles, central to which was the image of the Walrus, which John Lennon freely adapted from the Victorian surrealism of Lewis Carroll.

The concept of the mystery tour, touring the countryside in a multi-coloured bus, had much in common with a seminal "happening" in the annals of the American drug culture – the 1966 LSD-fed trip of Ken Kesey's Merry Pranksters in a day-glo bus, documented in Tom Wolfe's *Electric Kool Aid*

Acid Test. But whereas Kesey's Pranksters were for real, and their ports of call were rock concerts (including, incidentally, the Beatles) the Mystery Tour was a fiction, the passengers jolly day trippers in the English tradition. Situations visited included an Army recruitment centre, an Italian restaurant and a Busby Berkley style musical set – again nostalgia was a strong theme, alongside George's inner-looking multi-image piece and Lennon's inspired Walrus sequence. Although the latter provided the main "logo" for the record/book of *Magical Mystery Tour*, the imagery of the actual song was far richer than the animal-costumes-and-eggmen romping around in the film.

EMI Records

Photographs from *Magical Mystery Tour* which appeared in the "pages" of the album cover.

The "I am the walrus" sequence from *Magical Mystery Tour*

Baby You're A Rich Man

Coincidental with the release of *Magical Mystery Tour* came the opening of the Apple Shop at 94 Baker Street in London. This was the first practical manifestation of what was to become the Beatles' short-lived Apple empire, and stylistically – as a clothes boutique – the most pertinent to the times. Paul McCartney described it as "a beautiful place where you could buy beautiful things" (the word "beautiful" incidentally, seemed to be used as liberally and loosely as "love" in the era of the flower people). The main designs on sale were the work of a Dutch foursome who operated under the title of The Fool, and were the ultimate in "rich hippy" extravagance (as opposed to "ethnic" hippy where ideally the clothes would be home-made). The fairy-tale mix of oriental, medieval and even Red Indian styles made for a heady visual brew upon entering the shop, the outside of which was covered in a technicolour mural of swirling rainbows, planets and the other ephemera of psychedelic imagery.

The Apple boutique – which closed the following July with the celebrated "give away" event when the public were invited to come and take what they wanted – was the prelude to the setting up of Apple as an overall organisation.

As well as being the Beatles' own record label, Apple was to be an "open house" facility for any seemingly worthy artistic endeavour that might (often literally) knock on the door. The whole set up was highly vulnerable to charlatans and opportunists from the start; the Beatles, in a delirium of idealism brought on by the combined effects of drugs, meditation and sheer naivity, didn't see it that way of course. Like the boutique, most of the projects patronised by the Beatles through Apple didn't last long; the history of the decline of Apple is the history of the final couple of years of the Beatles as a group. "…we were an experiment in business operations…we were fresh and we were green…and when they said we were rotten and going broke, they were wrong. We were not. We were going right. All we wanted was more consistency and a visionary with a business brain at the top (rather than four visionaries growing up and apart painfully and publicly). We should have relaxed more. We had plenty of money (Apple never did go broke) and we had plenty of gifted people working there or offering to work with us. We were very short of time and we began to panic…"(From *As Time Goes By*, Derek Taylor, 1973.)

Only the record label was a financial success, still linked to EMI, and with the world-wide rights to all subsequent Beatles and much post-Beatles product, how could it be otherwise?

And it was the record label itself that provided another cipher in the now rich catalogue of Beatles' symbolism; for the rest of their collective existence, the Apple logo was synonymous with the Beatles. Based on a work by the surrealist painter, René Magritte – owned by Paul McCartney at the time – and designed by Gene Mahon, the label featured a whole apple on the A side of the records, a sliced apple on the B side – the first release was in August 1968, the Beatles' *Hey Jude*.

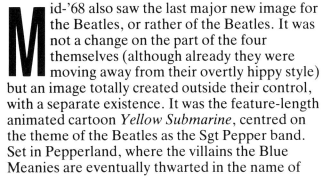

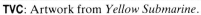

Yellow Submarine

Mid-'68 also saw the last major new image for the Beatles, or rather of the Beatles. It was not a change on the part of the four themselves (although already they were moving away from their overtly hippy style) but an image totally created outside their control, with a separate existence. It was the feature-length animated cartoon *Yellow Submarine*, centred on the theme of the Beatles as the Sgt Pepper band. Set in Pepperland, where the villains the Blue Meanies are eventually thwarted in the name of

TVC: Artwork from *Yellow Submarine*.

"Love Love Love", it was a classic fairy tale, a modern morality story and the final expression of the whimsical side of "love and peace".

Producer Al Brodax had begun the project in 1967, and through early 1968 the film was created using over five million separated sketches, by the London-based TVC (Television Cartoons) under John Coates, which had made the US TV cartoon series a couple of years earlier. Based on artwork by German poster artist ("poster" artist now being recognized as a function in its own right) Heinz Edelmann, the image created was a cartoon caricature of the popular concept of the post-Pepper Beatles – moustached, slightly foppish dandies but with the same earthy repartee in one-liners that they had spun off in *A Hard Day's Night* (although on this occasion, neither the script nor the dubbed-over voices were the Beatles' own).

The whole film reflected most of the visual styles fashionable in 1968, a sort of animated Alan Aldridge (in fact Aldridge was involved in early drawings for the project). A mixture of "art nouveau and psychedelia, op and pop, Dada and surrealist, Hieronymous Bosch and just plain bosh" was how one American review described it.

Despite the exotic mix of styles, much in the film was brilliantly conceived and executed. The "brushstroke" animation in the "Lucy in the Sky" sequence, the opening collage of Liverpool street photography, the bold use of typography to spell out *All You Need Is Love* – all stuck in the mind long after the story line had faded and become blurred.

Yellow Submarine was an enormous commercial success, and was significant in launching another wave of Beatle-oriented merchandising. More geared to the strictly junior market than previous Beatles ephemera, "Submarine" products were dominated by toys, games, puzzles and picture books. The entire project represented the final deliberate marketing of the Beatles as pop product.

TVC Ltd

TVC: Artwork from *Yellow Submarine*. ☞

TVC: Preliminary sketches and artwork from *Yellow Submarine*.

TVC: Artwork from *Yellow Submarine*.

TVC: Artwork from *Yellow Submarine*.

TVC: Artwork from *Yellow Submarine*.

Thoughts Meander Like A Restless Wind

Almost as if in reaction to the fictional face of the Beatles presented in "Submarine", the latter half of 1968 was when the "real" Beatles' image – warts and all – was made apparent as a part of group policy. It was to herald the group's gradual disintegration as a unit over the following year, but in 1968, with the success of singles *Lady Madonna* and *Hey Jude* and the *Yellow Submarine* film behind them, it merely appeared as another phase in the Beatles' chameleon-like history.

Despite these cooperative successes, the Beatles were actually spending far more time on individual projects; George had emerged as film composer with *Wonderwall*, while John's *In His Own Write* opened in a one-act version by the National Theatre at London's Old Vic. And the relatively candid revelations in the authorised biography by Hunter Davies, published in September 1968, emphasising the individuals in the group, seemed part of this process, as indeed did their end-of-the-year double album, entitled simply *The Beatles*.

Earlier in the year, John Lennon – under the new influence of his relationship with Yoko Ono – had staged a London art exhibition at the Robert Frazer Gallery of his "white art". Called *You Are*

Iain Macmillan: The display of charity collection boxes, a feature of John Lennon's "You Are Here" exhibition at the Robert Frazer Gallery, July 1968.

Here, the show consisted of items like a huge circular white canvas with "you are here" appearing microscopically, and a machine that continuously inflated white balloons to be released over London with "you are here" labels attached. All this was very much in line with the conceptual and minimalist art that the Japanese avant gardist Ono promoted.

Born in 1933, the daughter of a Tokyo banker, Yoko Ono grew up an academically bright but socially closeted teenager; when she eventually broke away from the traditional lifestyle of the Japanese upper class – by now in her twenties – she settled in New York where, after much perseverance, she became known among the art cognoscenti for her "happenings".

She was not unique in this, of course. New York painters – Allan Kaprow in particular – had extended the three-dimensional assemblage into mixed media "environmental" pieces, often involving live performance and/or audience participation. In Liverpool, this was taken up in the early '60s by Adrian Henri in a series of "events" that involved beat groups for the first time, and also provided a launching pad for the embryo poetry scene.

What marked the "happenings" of Yoko Ono, however, was their minimalism, their reliance on concept rather than on form. Where Kaprow and Henri *added* layers of experience – painting-with-music-with-poetry-with-movement – Ono's pieces were stripped to the bare *idea*. A blank canvas might be displayed for the audience to paint – *that* was the happening; another concert was said to have involved listening to boiling water evaporate.

Many of these concepts appeared in Yoko Ono's book *Grapefruit* – a list of conceptual instructions that appeared in 1964 but was being written from the mid-'50s. Many of the pieces instruct one to "imagine.." ("imagine a flower made of hard material...", "imagine dividing the canvas into twenty different shapes..."), a notion that John Lennon would incorporate into song years later.

By the mid-'60s, with her second husband Tony Cox as "manager" and general hustler, she had become something of a name outside New York; so much so that in 1966 she and her family (she had a daughter, Kyoko, by Cox) had settled in London.

The now legendary meeting between John and Yoko took place in November 1966 at the fashionable Indica Gallery. Under the auspices of Barry Miles, among others, the Indica had enjoyed a certain amount of patronage from the Beatles –

Catalogue, with photograph by Iain Macmillan, for the "Yoko At Indica" exhibition, November 1966.

at one stage, the Indica bookshop even had its wrapping paper designed by Paul McCartney. Yoko had an exhibition at the gallery, and John was invited to the preview (by the Indica rather than by Yoko, who, while being aware of the Beatles – and who couldn't be in 1966 – was not particularly concerned with them or their music). Lennon's first encounter with Yoko involved his hammering an imaginary nail into one of her canvasses for an imaginary five shillings. Out of such an acorn acquaintance came the solid-as-oak relationship, mental as much as physical, that was to influence Lennon's work so profoundly in the coming years.

While Lennon always commented that "*avant garde* was French for bullshit", the Yoko Ono approach to art neatly coincided with – and helped to rationalise – his own gut instinct, which was always in favour of inspiration rather than technique as the prime criterion for creative activity. All the way through his career – from his art school days, when he had ignored "real" painting in favour of off-the-cuff cartoons and had maintained his faith in Stuart Sutcliffe as a musician because he had had the right "attitude", to his "stream of consciousness" surrealism and eventual promotion of Yoko's seemingly minimal musical abilities – Lennon's inclination was to let instinct, intuition and inspiration rule; the rest would follow. With the partnership of the more workmanlike McCartney and the inbuilt discipline of writing for a working group, follow it usually did; without such constraints, John's work, while frequently brilliant, included a proportion that was at best immemorable, at worst incomprehensible – an accusation that could rarely be levied at the music of the Beatles.

Apart from the influence it had on Lennon's music, the most immediate effect of his involvement with Yoko Ono was to lead him to branch out into hitherto non-Beatle areas of the art world – hence the "white art" exhibition with its preoccupation with minimalism and conceptualism – ideas that were clearly reflected in the stark packaging of *The Beatles*, referred to almost immediately after its release as the "white album".

Iain Macmillan

Iain Macmillan: Exhibits from the "Yoko At Indica" exhibition, including (bottom row, ☞ second from left) the piece which brought together Lennon and Ono for the first time.

The "White" Album

Richard Hamilton: Insert collage for the "White Album".

Richard Hamilton/EMI Records

Beatles album sleeves, in the mind of the group itself as much as in the opinion of fawning fans and critics, had now assumed the status of Works of Art. *Revolver* established this, and "Pepper" confirmed it. Before *Revolver*, the album packaging had been in the traditional nature of a promotional exercise. Although the covers, dominated by the photography of Robert Freeman, had each broken new ground, they still served to promote the image of the Beatles, and became in doing so the visual beacons to the development of their style as well as their music.

The "white" album, on the other hand, was the ultimate – and final – "art" album sleeve, minimalist in its plain white with "The Beatles" embossed subtly, and conceptual in that the Beatles decided that the first two million copies should bear individual "edition" numbers.

Inside the sleeve, however, there was ample concession to a more representational approach, with the inclusion of four colour photographs and a collage composition by Richard Hamilton – one of the British pop painters who had largely shunned home-grown subject matter in favour of Americana in the late '50s and early '60s.

Like the portraits inserted, Hamilton's collage serves to emphasise the group as individuals, the snapshots, polaroids and strips of contact prints are predominantly of single Beatles – only a couple of shots of them as a group occur.

The "warts and all" aspect of the album was in the music; not only did it signify the emergence of the Beatles as individuals, in that often three merely acted as "rhythm section" to the one who was performing "his" song, or in some cases didn't play at all. The by-line "Lennon and McCartney" was now largely an empty formality – John and Paul and increasingly George, wrote their "own" songs. Many, including producer Martin, also felt the album over-long, that it included half-perfected numbers that could have been shelved for later release, leaving a single album of greater strength and unity.

Only Trying To Get Us Some Peace

Recording apart, the Beatles were together less frequently than ever before in their life as a group. Business "conferences" would be held from time to time at a chaotic Apple office, but the times when all four were sufficiently well organised to be in the same place at the same time were few and far between. The outward public image of the group as a unit was perpetuated by organised photosessions, usually with eminent photographers. Donald McCullin, already a world-renowned news photographer by the late '60s, was commissioned to spend the day with the group in this way, and out of this came the eventual centre-fold to EMI's *1962-66* and *1967-70* compilations. One of McCullin's pictures was also used years later as the basis for Liverpool painter Maurice Cockrill's two paintings of the Beatles.

The most prolific photographer of the group during this period, for obvious reasons, was Paul McCartney's girl-friend and soon-to-be wife, Linda Eastman. She was already making a name for herself in New York as a photographer of the rock

Linda McCartney: George Harrison.

Centre spread of *The Beatles 1962-66* compilation album, with a photograph by Donald McCullin.

SIDE 1
LOVE ME DO
(Lennon & McCartney)
PLEASE PLEASE ME
(Lennon & McCartney)
FROM ME TO YOU
(Lennon & McCartney)
SHE LOVES YOU
(Lennon & McCartney)
I WANT TO HOLD YOUR HAND
(Lennon & McCartney)
ALL MY LOVING
(Lennon & McCartney)
CAN'T BUY ME LOVE
(Lennon & McCartney)

SIDE 2
A HARD DAY'S NIGHT
(Lennon & McCartney)
AND I LOVE HER
(Lennon & McCartney)
EIGHT DAYS A WEEK
(Lennon & McCartney)
I FEEL FINE
(Lennon & McCartney)
TICKET TO RIDE
(Lennon & McCartney)
YESTERDAY
(Lennon & McCartney)

SIDE 3
HELP!
(Lennon & McCartney)
YOU'VE GOT TO HIDE YOUR LOVE AWAY
(Lennon & McCartney)
WE CAN WORK IT OUT
(Lennon & McCartney)
DAY TRIPPER
(Lennon & McCartney)
DRIVE MY CAR
(Lennon & McCartney)
NORWEGIAN WOOD (THIS BIRD HAS FLOWN)
(Lennon & McCartney)

SIDE 4
NOWHERE MAN
(Lennon & McCartney)
MICHELLE
(Lennon & McCartney)
IN MY LIFE
(Lennon & McCartney)
GIRL
(Lennon & McCartney)
PAPERBACK WRITER
(Lennon & McCartney)
ELEANOR RIGBY
(Lennon & McCartney)
YELLOW SUBMARINE
(Lennon & McCartney)

All titles produced by George Martin

Linda McCartney: John and Yoko.

Linda McCartney: Paul and his dog Martha.

fraternity, and her work with the Beatles and others was becoming a regular feature of *Rolling Stone* magazine. Her first book, after she became Mrs McCartney, was called *Linda's Pictures* and consisted of a cross section of her work at this time.

On March 12th 1969 Paul married Linda Eastman, and just eight days later John married Yoko Ono; while both events, particularly the latter, were to be blamed by public and pundits alike for the disbandment of the group, the Ono-Lennon partnership was certainly to create the most controversy in terms of their subsequent artistic ventures.

The most public manifestations of John and Yoko's conceptualism were the notorious "bag-ins" for peace that were part-happening, part-propaganda and part-publicity stunt, culminating in the week-long "bed-in" at the Amsterdam Hilton at the time of their honeymoon. Curiously, although the "happening" was all-important at the time, of much more permanent value are drawings Lennon did while on honeymoon, reminiscent of his zany cartoons of earlier years.

Less innocent drawings were to come with the publication of the *Bag One* limited edition of erotic lithographs where Lennon illustrated graphically his relationship with Yoko. This too had to be an event, of course, so the drawings were published in a white plastic bag, hence the title. Other less accessible aspects of the Lennons' conceptual art of the time included acorns-for-peace events, a "self portrait" film in which John filmed his own penis for 42 minutes, and the assortment of ill-received records released by John and Yoko before and during the months immediately after their marriage.

The combined effects of the various Beatles' private activities, and of the apparent disunity in the group as a whole led to a growing desire among their fans – and the world at large, which had for a time during the mid-'60s taken the Beatles (or at least the image of the Beatles) to its heart – for a return to the "old" Beatles. This very real feeling was to dictate the nature of the Beatles' final months of activity as a unit, and to dominate the way in which their image has been perpetuated visually ever since.

The disbandment of the Beatles as a group was crucial in the transition of their image from that of present day superstars to symbols of an aspect of history. Even if the Rolling Stones, the Beatles' nearest rivals in many respects, had acquired as strong an image in symbolic terms during the '60s (and, of course, they didn't), the mere fact that they stayed together – on however irregular a basis – would have ruled out similar developments.

Much of the art of the Beatles that appeared in the '70s – and even more so, after Lennon's assassination, during the '80s – simply would not have occurred had the group not broken up. But break up it did, despite efforts on their part to get back to aspects of their former glory; aspects reflected in the music and concepts apparent in their final two albums, *Abbey Road* and *Let It Be*. *Let It Be* (actually recorded before *Abbey Road* but released later) sought to capture the live spontaneity of a rehearsal session without the discipline or technical sophistication of George Martin's involvement: *Abbey Road* on the other hand, was a deliberate attempt to recapture – with Martin back in the producer's chair – the highly crafted essence of their recording successes of the past.

Linda McCartney: Ringo Starr.

Abbey Road

Iain Macmillan/EMI Records

A retreat from the self-consciously "arty" covers of *Revolver*, *Sgt Pepper* and the "white" album, the sleeve and title of *Abbey Road* represented a contrived but uncomplicated acknowledgement of the scene of their greatest artistic achievements, the Abbey Road EMI recording studio. Although the existence of preliminary sketches by Paul McCartney suggests that the "zebra crossing" photograph was his idea, photographer Iain Macmillan recalls that it was much more the result of general agreement. The setting had no special significance at the time, but once it had appeared on the sleeve, it became another – in fact the last – in the long line of strong Beatles images perpetuated through their album sleeves.

Appearing in the autumn of 1969, at the time of the "Paul is dead" rumours sweeping America, the cover also took on an added symbolic significance never intended in what was a straightforward idea for a simple cover picture. The fact that Paul McCartney was walking barefoot, with Lennon wearing a white suit, was all seen as evidence of the hoax, constructed by the remaining three Beatles, to cover up McCartney's death by replacing him with a look-alike.

The erstwhile clue-spotters would have had a field day could they have seen Macmillan's other photographs from the zebra crossing session, with the Beatles assuming various enigmatic positions on the now cryptic thoroughfare – the Beatles walking right to left, for example (why the change in order?), the zebra crossing empty (now *that* could have signified all sorts of calamities). Every change, every nuance – George smiling on that one, a vehicle moved on another – could have been another "clue", if clues it was you sought.

The image immediately became as lasting as that of the other Beatles' album sleeves, and over the next decade lent itself to pun and parody of various kinds – a sure sign of a truly universal visual concept.

The record marked the final statement by the Beatles as a group, combining some of their finest writing as individuals (George particularly excelled with *Here Comes The Sun* and *Something*), with a largely Paul-inspired medley of songs, running one into the other on the second side. The whole album highlighted a new instrumental excellence on the part of all four Beatles, Ringo even getting a drum solo! Like Macmillan's cover photography, *Abbey Road* was technically brilliant, coolly inspired, and bound to last.

Abbey Road, while in fact being the Beatles' final recorded work together, was not the last to reach the ears of the general public; their epitaph – for that is what it became – was the long-delayed *Let It Be*.

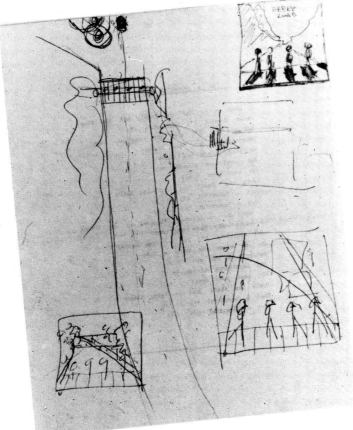

Iain Macmillan

Paul McCartney: The original sketches for the *Abbey Road* cover, photographed by Iain Macmillan.

Iain Macmillan: One of the series of *Abbey Road* shots that produced the classic cover.

Let It Be

Originally to be titled *Get Back*, a clue to the album's aim of returning to the group's musical base, *Let It Be* took the form of an "unrehearsed" studio session, recorded on film as well as tape. The cover, when the album was recorded prior to *Abbey Road* in 1969, was – on John Lennon's suggestion – to have been a *déja vu* version of Angus McBean's *Please Please Me* cover of 1963, again by McBean, with the group – bearded or moustached – taking up the same positions looking over the famous stairwell.

After much wrangling and delay, the album (re-mixed in part by Phil Spector) was released in 1970, along with the film, which provided a disturbing commentary on the much-publicised break-up of the group by then taking place – it was not immediately apparent to most of the film's audience that the sessions had been filmed over a year before.

Bordered in black, the album cover otherwise followed very traditional pop album convention – just the title with four (separate) pictures of the Beatles. The release initially took the form of a package, another "event", with a glossy book of photographs by Ethan Russell taken at the sessions being included in a boxed set. Ironically, the early print deadline meant that the books were all called *Get Back* while the album was now renamed *Let It Be*. After the first few thousand, *Let It Be* appeared (at a conventional price) minus the book.

The music of *Let It Be* was at times as inspired as anything the Beatles had done, but the absence of George Martin showed through on the production side. Design-wise, the cover had little to offer, although the film – and book – did capture the last memorable visual image of the Beatles; on the wind-swept roof of the Apple office, during the *Get Back* sequence, after which Lennon closed the performance, the album and (unwittingly) the Beatles' contribution to musical history, with the typically anti-climactic "…thank you from all the group, and I hope we passed the audition."

Angus McBean's *déja vu* stairwell session did eventually appear on record sleeves, as part of the cover (along with a picture from the original *Please Please Me* session) of EMI's *1962-66* and *1967-70* compilations. The fact that these were put together (in 1973) and became huge sellers in their own right, was testament to the lasting appeal of the Beatles. It was an appeal that was lasting in more senses than one. The image of the Beatles during the years since their disbandment has come to represent, even more so than it did during the '60s, a great many things, and to function in a number of ways. No other figures from the post-war years, and certainly none ever from popular music, has had a "posthumous" image that came to mean so many things to so many people, was used by artists and designers in so many different ways. Elvis Presley may have epitomised rock'n'roll, as did Marilyn Monroe Hollywood glamour, and both of them the '50s years. But the Beatles captured much more – the feel, the style, the *attitudes* of an era; they are attitudes that many would still identify with, and for which the Beatles have remained the essential symbol.

Angus McBean: The return to the "stairwell" setting, intended for the cover of *Get Back* before it was renamed *Let It Be*. ☞

Picture disc released as part of EMI's "It Was Twenty Years Ago" campaign.

Yesterday

The years since the passing of the Beatles have seen a proliferation of images – two dimensional and otherwise – perpetuating the memory of a group which, in reality, ceased to exist a decade and a half ago. So strong was their influence at the time, and so durable their musical and nostalgic appeal, that they have become the universally accepted symbols for the era of the '60s. And as people's perception of the era has changed with the passage of time, so has the "art" of the Beatles undergone a series of transitions. The image has acquired its own dynamic; it has not been allowed to stagnate. Since 1970, there has been more creative activity using the Beatles as source material than there ever was when they formed a creative group themselves.

While the Beatles have become symbols and subject matter throughout the world of the visual arts, their image has also continued to function as the basis for a whole post-Beatles industry, feeding the demand created by their continuing popularity. "Industry" in this sense does not mean simply a production line of commemorative memorabilia or instant nostalgia – although there has been an inevitable element of that – but a flow of books, plays, films, cartoons, even parodies and send-ups, all of which have used, adapted and often extended the overall visual image of the Beatles.

The flow of such material has accelerated over the years; realisation that the Beatles were no more was not immediate. Months passed, then years, while the faithful continued to hope that they might get together again. As that hope faded, so the Beatles passed into history, to be chronicled, analysed and celebrated in a way that was impossible while they were still together. And any lingering hopes of even a one-off Beatles "reunion" were shattered with the death of John Lennon in December 1980. John was dead – the Beatles were dead.

Its A Thousand Pages
Give Or Take A Few

In addition to the inevitable fan-oriented pulp biographies that flooded the market from the years of Beatlemania onwards, there had been a steady trickle of more serious literature dating from those same years in the '60s when it became obvious that the Beatles were a phenomenon without precedent in the history of pop. Early volumes of note include the now-classic *Love Me Do: The Beatles' Progress* by Michael Braun, an account of life on the road with the group at the height of the 1964 Beatle boom; an American collection of fan letters entitled *Love Letters To The Beatles* by Bill Adler; and Brian Epstein's autobiographical *Cellarful Of Noise* ghost written by Derek Taylor. All these appeared in 1964 when the group's success in America ensured that their every move was charted and chronicled for posterity.

The Beatles' history was institutionalised in 1968 with the Hunter Davies "authorised" biography, done with the cooperation of the group. Their involvement, while allowing greater accuracy, also guaranteed that it was the "official" account rather than the definitive history.

The end of the decade saw the publication of the *Illustrated Lyrics* by Alan Aldridge, representing the most significant single development in the role of illustrators and designers in Beatles literature – a role that was to increase through the '70s as the Beatles themselves became a thing of the past.

The flood of written material about the Beatles – although inevitable with their demise – was greatly increased by the fact that it was part of a general explosion of rock literature as a whole. By the mid-'70s, rock had come of age. It was twenty-one years since Elvis Presley had made his historic debut records in Memphis, Tennessee; two decades that had seen rock influence not just the course of popular music, but society itself. Ironically, the recognition that popular music had a history – and one which was important both for its own sake and as a part of social history – came at a time when the music itself was, arguably, at an-all time low. Rock had polarised: "serious"

rock had got too serious for its own good, pretentious for a music which in essence was simple, intuitive and accessible. "Pop" rock on the other hand – partly as a reaction to the "progressives" – had become totally trivialised. Despite the efforts of some noble exceptions, David Bowie and Roxy Music among them, there was no force uniting both wings, no figureheads leading and popularising at the same time......no Beatles.

In this climate, many looked back to the history of the music, which now had enough substance to satisfy anyone who cared to investigate. The time of the rock writer had arrived, and with it a consequent proliferation of rock illustration.

The Aldridge books were pioneering examples of what in the '70s was to become the norm in pop literature – the "coffee table" large format paperback; glossy, lavishly illustrated volumes in which the pictures were as important as, if not more important than, the words. A prime example was *Rock Dreams* (1974) by artist Guy Peelaert and writer Nik Cohn, a book of illustrations featuring the heroes of rock (including the Beatles) in surreal and sometimes outrageous situations. Rock art had become recognised, alongside rock literature, as part of contemporary culture.

Early in the '70s, as soon as it became clear that the Beatles were no more, the first of the many "looking back" volumes appeared. This particular book consisted of a series of candid interviews with John Lennon conducted by Jann Wenner of *Rolling Stone* magazine, and published in England by Penguin Books as *Lennon Remembers*. During the 1960s, Penguin had moved away from the standardised "utility" covers with minimal illustration that had characterised their books in the '40s and '50s, and had acquired a reputation for highly original covers – a case in point being the Aldridge-designed cover for their one-volume edition of the two Lennon books (*The Penguin John Lennon*) in 1966. *Lennon Remembers* belonged very much to this trend, with an intriguing "back-and-front" cover illustration by

Alan Aldridge

Alan Aldridge

Alan Aldridge: Covers for Hunter Davies' *The Beatles: The Authorised Biography* and Aldridge's *Illustrated Lyrics*.

Philip Castle: Cover illustration for *Lennon Remembers*.

Philip Castle, one of the originators of the "air-brush" technique in commercial illustration.

More Beatle-based reminiscences came in 1973 with Derek Taylor's memories of days at Apple and elsewhere in *As Time Goes By*, while an insight into the Beatles' early years in Liverpool and Hamburg appeared with *The Man Who Gave The Beatles Away* by their first manager Alan Williams (he of the title) and journalist William Marshall.

Of more interest visually, in that they either perpetuated the Beatles' image or adapted it in some way, was a wave of books that appeared in the late '70s and early '80s. Bill Harry's celebrated *Merseybeat* newspaper was recalled graphically in *Merseybeat: The Beginning Of The Beatles*, a volume of reproductions of pages from the paper, concentrating on articles and news items about the Beatles and including John Lennon's contributions in his *Beatcomber* column.

The same year (1978) saw the publication of the first book to come out of the real "inner circle" of the Beatles, their family and friends. It was *A Twist Of Lennon*, the punning title of the memoirs of John Lennon's first wife Cynthia, who had by this time become Cynthia Twist. A major feature of Cynthia's book was the inclusion of a collection of line drawings, giving a highly personal view of the public and private aspects of the Beatles saga. Often intentionally funny, they included the Beatles at the Cavern, with the Maharishi, Cynthia in the maternity hospital, and escaping (under a raincoat with John) down a hotel corridor.

The lavishly illustrated Rolling Stone publication *The Beatles* came out (in both paperback *and* hardback, the latter becoming something of a rarity in large format pop books) in 1980. Written by Geoffrey Stokes, with a prestigious introduction by Leonard Bernstein, it boasted a cover by pop artist Andy Warhol – based on photographs taken by Dezo Hoffmann in 1963 – which, in the hardback edition, minus the typography, doubled as a poster.

The death of John Lennon at the end of 1980 brought a rash of Beatle books, and purely John Lennon books. Many of these were "quickie" dedications, but Philip Norman's *Shout* – which he had been preparing some time *before* Lennon's death – stood out as the nearest to a definitive history of the Beatles yet to appear. Meticulously researched, and written with considerable sensitivity for the feeling of the times it describes, *Shout* appeared initially with a cover that utilised the familiar "With The Beatles" Robert Freeman

Penguin Books

Cynthia Lennon: "Brian Is Dead, Long Live Brian" – the Beatles and entourage with the Maharishi, from *A Twist Of Lennon* (Star Books)

James Marsh: Cover illustration for *Shout* by Philip Norman, 1982.

photograph, confirming it as a classic – perhaps *the* classic – image of the group. The subsequent paperback edition, however, carried a cover by illustrator James Marsh, a fantasy-land picture of the Sgt Pepper Beatles standing in a field of strawberries, ladybirds buzzing around their heads.

As the mythification of the Beatles continued, representations of them moved further and further from reality. James Marsh's faces of the group anticipated the development of an essentially simplistic style of illustration, related in part to trends away from abstraction in favour of figurative painting in non-commercial art. Typical of this "primitive" approach was the cover for Bill Harry's *Beatles Who's Who* (1982), by Yorkshire artist Steve Gublis. The Gublis painting had the group in various modes of attire, locked in their particular time warps – George the eternal hippy, John the Liverpool rocker, Paul the besuited mop top, and Ringo the grinning Sgt Pepper bandsman.

Purely illustrative volumes also appeared, particularly after Lennon's death, containing photographs of the Beatles that were now seen as social history rather than current pop – their original function. The two most prominent photographers of the group, Dezo Hoffmann and Robert Freeman, both published collections of their now historic work – Hoffmann in *With The Beatles* (1982) and Freeman with *Yesterday*, published in 1983.

Significantly, there have been few Beatle-based works of fiction over the years, perhaps because the reality is too familiar, both in its detail in the public mind and in its historical proximity – the Beatle legend is simply too "close". There were, however, two novels of interest published in the early '60s. Sean Hignett's *A Picture To Hang On The Wall* was set in the bohemia of Liverpool 8 at the beginning of the decade, a novel populated by painters and writers rather than beat musicians, but important all the same as an insight into the environment, centred on Ye Cracke, which was also the stomping ground of the embryo Beatles, Sutcliffe and Lennon.

More directly relevant to the Beatles, and certainly inspired by their success, was *All Night Stand*, by Thom Keyes, an American-born Liverpool writer. It traced the story of a four-piece Liverpool beat group from the cellar clubs to international fame, and although the parallel with the Beatles is clearly there, the novel was set at a time (1964) when other Liverpool groups were also making it world-wide. In fact, Keyes did most of

his on-the-road research with Faron's Flamingos, who never found national or international fame, and with the Searchers, who did.

No reference to the literature of the Beatles would be complete without mentioning *The Beatles* published in 1971 by minimalist poet Aram Saroyan, which sold at five cents a copy and consisted of eight words over four pages, each poem being simply the name of a Beatle!

Steve Gublis: Painting for the cover of *The Beatles Who's Who* by Bill Harry (Aurum Press).

Lend Me Your Ears And I'll
Sing You A Song

EMI Records

EMI Records

THE BEATLES AT THE HOLLYWOOD BOWL

Central to the post-Beatles industry, of course, was the release (or in most cases re-release) of records. Although none of their '60s output was deleted by EMI, and no fresh studio material lay in the vaults (at least none that they were in a position to release) the company managed to repackage tracks in a number of compilation albums during the '70s. The first of these were the *Beatles 1962-66* and *1967-70* double LP collections of 1973, which were purely "historic" in their approach. Subsequent compilations adopted a thematic approach, covering *Rock'n'Roll Music*, *Ballads*, *Love Songs* and *Rarities* – plus a set of "cleaned up" live recordings *The Beatles At The Hollywood Bowl*, the only "new" material to appear.

Of concern here, however, is the way in which the image of the Beatles was reflected in these exercises. An obvious complement to repackaged tracks would be a repackaged version of their established image – which is indeed what happened on the *1962-66* and *1967-70* collections, with the 1963 and 1969 *déja vu* stairwell photographs by Angus McBean. Similarly, the *Love Songs* collection used the 1967 Richard Avedon pictures originally commissioned by *Look* magazine (with Paul and Ringo's positions changed), and the *Hollywood Bowl* album featured a collection of memorabilia – concert tickets, programmes, pennants and badges – from the period.

Two of the compilations carried original artwork. *Rock'n'Roll Music* featured the work of an American illustrator Ignacio Gomez, the front and back of the sleeve depicting the front and back of the group, with the thumb and fingers of someone holding the album as part of the illustration – very strange. The gatefold sleeve opened up to a more conventional montage of '50s images – Coca Cola, cars and the obligatory Marilyn Monroe.

More interesting in many ways was the cover for *Beatles Ballads* by John Patrick Byrne; showing the Beatles as wide-eyed nursery animals, the cover was a studied version of the naive style of the

EMI Records

Detail from the centre spread of the *Love Songs* compilation (see also above), featuring a picture by Richard Avedon.

The *Beatles Ballads* compilation, with cover painting by Patrick Byrne.

French primitive artist, Henri Rousseau. Byrne was responsible for several well-known album covers during the '70s, perhaps the most familiar being that for the *Stealer's Wheel* album and later for Gerry Rafferty, again in a similar style.

The other proliferation of recorded material was of course in the area of "bootlegged" and other non-EMI tracks. The artwork for these covers was drawn largely from standard images of the group, depending on the period concerned. The only non-pirates in this output were the continual repackagings of the recordings made by the Beatles in their early days in Hamburg. These too have appeared under a number of labels, with various album titles, and a variety of covers, again using photographs (usually unofficially) from the

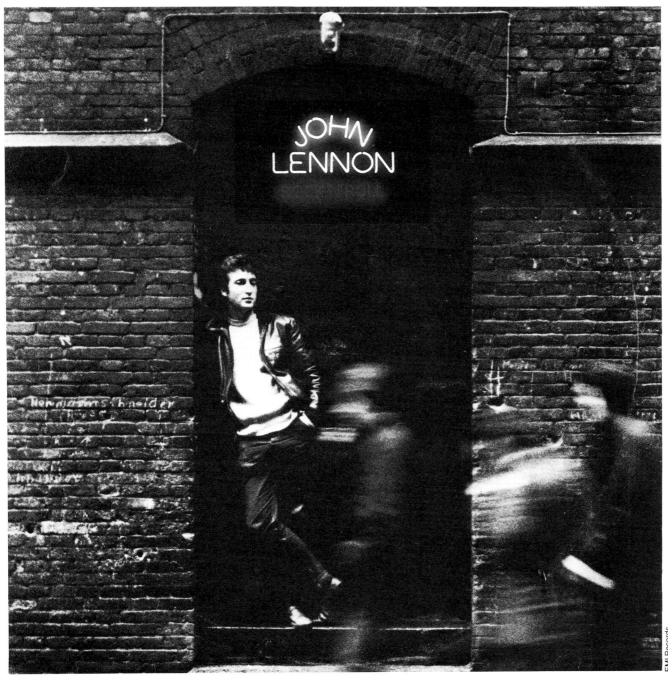

Cover for John Lennon's *Rock'n'Roll* album, with photograph by Jurgen Vollmer.

period. One "official" use of an early Hamburg shot came with the 1975 Apple release of the John Lennon album *Rock'n'Roll*. These were new recordings by John of the old-time rock'n'roll favourites that he had played from the beginning of his career, and the cover was a vintage Hamburg shot of a leather-clad John taken in 1961 by Jurgen Vollmer, one of the art students who (along with Astrid Kirchherr and Klaus Voorman) had helped to create the original image of the Beatles. So even the earliest images of the group were getting recycled, although this was the only instance of a Beatles period picture being used on a post-Beatles album by one of the former fab four.

Everyman Theatre, Liverpool

Lyric Theatre

The Act You've Known For All These Years

Although the profit motive may have loomed large in the background to many of these post-Beatles enterprises, particularly the record releases, most were presented as either indispensable to a complete historical record of the group (in the case of bootlegs and "definitive" histories), or a straight "homage" to the group. Where the "homage" motive has seemed at its most genuine has been in the theatre – the chance of plays making money being minimal at the best of times.

The first of these productions came in 1974, and was certainly the most ambitious; an attempt to capture the story, the mood and the *feel* of the Beatles phenomenon in one work. Written by a Liverpool schoolteacher, Willy Russell, it opened at Liverpool's Everyman Theatre in 1974 under the odd-ball title of *John Paul George Ringo.....and Bert*. Bert of course represents the eternal Beatles fan, a one-time drummer with the group (like the legendary Tommy Moore who went back to his job at Garston Bottle Works after a couple of gigs) who acts as narrator throughout.

The play came at a time when the Everyman was gaining a strong reputation among English provincial theatres, and in retrospect the cast included some formidable names. Anthony Sher, more recently known for such stage and television roles as *The History Man* played Ringo and designed the poster for the play. Paul McCartney was played by Trevor Eve, latterly famous for his role in *Children Of A Lesser God* and as TV's Eddie Shoestring. Bernard Hill (Alan Bleasdale's " gizza job" Yosser Hughes in *The Boys From The Blackstuff*) was John Lennon, while the musical continuity was provided by Barbara Dickson.

Rather than employ a guitar-and-drums group, performing what would inevitably be considered "second hand" versions of the originals, Russell had Dickson – a singer/pianist from the folk club circuit – performing with a rhythm section in a virtually solo capacity, changing the texture of the music to such a degree that comparison with the original was pointless. Tempos were changed for dramatic effect – the lyrics of *Help* for instance took on an added poignancy at slow tempo, perhaps giving the effect that Lennon had originally intended – and familiar songs revealed hidden possibilities rather than being "watered down" in the process.

The play was highly successful, moving to a West End run at London's Lyric Theatre, establishing Russell as a writer (he went on to further successes, the best-known so far being *Educating Rita*) and Barbara Dickson as a recording artist.

The Everyman Theatre was also responsible for *Lennon*, a play by Bob Eaton which appeared after John's death, in 1981. It moved to an off-Broadway run in New York with no great success: the Equity ruling that work should go to local (in other words American) actors was thought to have had something to do with it. An amusing anecdote arises from *Lennon*'s short run in America. Some months after it had closed, Arthur Ballard, visiting his son in New York, was introduced to an out-of-work actor at a party who mentioned that his last audition had been for the part of "some old guy who taught John Lennon at Art College", not realising that he was talking to the original.

Stu, based on "scenes from the life of Stuart Sutcliffe" first appeared in a small theatre outside London (in Bromley, Kent) in September 1983. Written by Jeremy Stockwell and Hugh O'Neill, it featured Paul Almond in a one-man performance of the crucial (and best documented) episodes from Sutcliffe's life. For a theme that had seemingly essential supporting parts (if only those of Astrid and John Lennon), the play was surprisingly successful, and the solo delivery of short scenes kept the focus on Sutcliffe rather than his charismatic girlfriend and larger-than-life colleague.

Of the other theatrical productions based on the Beatles, an American-inspired venture called *Beatlemania* by Jules Fisher was doomed to artistic failure for reasons that mirror those that made the plays cited above successful in their own different ways. It was an attempt to capture the "authentic" sound and feel of the Beatles and their era, with a look-alike group and a singing-and-dancing supporting cast. Financially, the show apparently did well in the United States, where it opened on Broadway in May 1977, but it made only a short-lived impression in London.

Similarly fated – and for entirely different reasons – was a Robert Stigwood extravaganza *Sgt Pepper's Lonely Hearts Club Band On The Road* which had opened on Broadway in 1974 (with,

amazingly, the token approval of John Lennon) and became, in 1977, the feature film *Sgt Pepper's Lonely Hearts Club Band*. Using the talents of then US teenybop idols Peter Frampton and the Bee Gees, Stigwood managed to create a grotesque circus of the lowest common denominator of American youth-oriented middle-of-the-road pop, a million miles from anything representing the Beatles – except for the title.

Two other movie projects were rather more agreeable – both as reflections of some aspects of the Beatles, and as works in themselves. *The Birth Of The Beatles* (1979), an American made-for-TV film shot mainly in England, managed to capture, with a certain sensitivity, the early '60s Liverpool and Hamburg of the Beatles. For those who remembered the reality, of course, it was full of inaccuracy; but for the vast majority, whose perceptions were based on received images from photographs and suchlike, it rang true – it *felt* right.

The other venture on film which also came over as feeling "right", albeit often in a completely over-the-top way, was a mid-'70s cinema feature called *I Want To Hold Your Hand*. Set in New York during the Beatles' debut visit there, as the nation awaited their appearance on the Ed Sullivan TV show, it followed the chaotic adventures of a group of fans determined to get to meet their idols, who were holed up in a Manhattan hotel. Apart from images on TV monitors as the Sullivan show is being broadcast, all we ever see of the Beatles is a shot of their cuban-heeled boots and trouser bottoms as they walk around the hotel bedroom, glimpsed from under a bed by one of the intrepid devotees.. But the film captured the excitement and euphoria of Beatlemania, against the aural backdrop of their music and the frantic screams of young America.

The reference to the Beatles (even indirectly as in the case of *Stu* and *I Want To Hold Your Hand*) in plays and films has served to feed the myth, strengthen the image and elevate their story to folk-lore. And the story of the Beatles had plainly acquired the status of folk-lore of a particularly 20th century kind when it appeared in comic strip form.

Goo Goo G'Joob

Marvel Comics

In the light of the other manifestations of Beatlemania in the mid-'60s, particularly in the United States, it is surprising that the Beatles never ended up in a syndicated comic strip, along with Flash Gordon, Mickey Mouse and Dagwood and Blondie. While they were together, they managed to avoid that fate, but when they became *history*, with a story that had a beginning, a middle *and* an end, they did feature in more than one picture-strip version of the familiar saga.

Apart from an American picture book for children in 1971, *We Love You Beatles*, it wasn't until 1978 that the Beatles story was run as a strip. It was published as a one-off "special" by the Marvel Comics group, who had by then become brand leaders in the comic book world, with such characters as the Incredible Hulk, Spiderman and the Fantastic Four, heirs apparent to the title of supreme superheroes which had been held in the '60s by Superman and Batman. The Beatle's story was something of a departure from the fantasy world inhabited by most of Marvel's output. However, it fitted comfortably into an established (in America) tradition of "real life" comics which had, in the 1950s, pioneered strip versions of literary classics (the *Classics Illustrated* series) and had later branched into strips based both on stories from history and on contemporary personalities in fictional situations (for example the Pat Boone comics). With the Beatles story, almost a fantasy in itself, Marvel were able to combine both of these ideas – a "true" history with real-life superheroes.

Much of the Marvel treatment was, unfortunately (and unintentionally) hilarious. Apart from the drawings, which could hardly be said to resemble any of the Beatles – and surely there were more pictures of the Beatles on which to base an accurate likeness than there were of anyone else on earth – some of the language and setting were risible to say the least. The basement cellar where the group first played with Pete Best, the Casbah Club, appears as some nightclubish establishment with lamps on each table – one is tempted to ask whether there were even tables in the place at all: Brian Epstein is portrayed as nothing less than a Hollywood heavy – if not a gangster, certainly a con-man – as he shuffles his way through rain-soaked Liverpool streets with his collar turned up and broad-brimmed trilby pulled well over his eyes: the Beatles talk to each other in phrases like "...hello mate, that's really gear..." and so on. Even the set pieces – Sgt Pepper, the roof session at Apple, are so badly executed it says something for the familiarity of the images that they are recognisable at all.

The Story Of The Beatles on the other hand, which was published in 1981 as a serial in the TV Times teenage spin-off *Look In*, was an entirely different matter. With a faithful version of the story and reasonably realistic dialogue by Angus P. Allen, the artwork – by Arthur Ranson – achieved a high degree of accuracy for comic book work. Based on familiar (and sometimes not-so-familiar) photographs, and aided by imaginative layouts that reflected the story line, it managed to suggest something of the dynamic of the Beatles' history. Important characters often omitted from more "comprehensive" histories – like Cavern DJ Bob Wooler who helped establish the Beatles in Liverpool before *and* after they signed with Brian Epstein – are not only included, but look right; something the Marvel edition failed to do even with the Beatles themselves.

The *Look In* serial was published as a one-off volume special in 1982. It remains the only worthwhile comic strip record of the Beatles.

stereo   **Guaranteed To Raise A Smile**

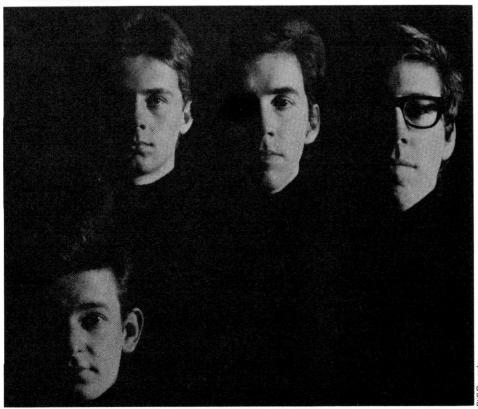

Cover of the *With The Roogalator* EP, 1977.

Where the comic strips were attempting to tell the story straight rather than to be "comic" as such (although Marvel achieved this by default), the various forms of lampoon and parody that appeared over the years all played on familiar Beatles images, sending them up with varying degrees of wit, affection and success. The main sources for parody were also the sources of the most lasting of these images – the album sleeves. From the late '60s, when Frank Zappa released *We're Only In It For The Money*, the Beatles' sleeves had become so universally known as to make any send up instantly obvious. The Zappa cover was, in fact, a parody of Sgt Pepper, with the leader and his Mothers of Invention sitting – in drag in his case – in front of a motley assembly of characters, ranging from Liberace's brother George to the Phantom of the Opera.

The omnipresent image of *With The Beatles* has had its share of imitators over the years, often groups adopting the side-lit technique for their own cover photographs, enough removed from the Freeman picture to avoid accusations of plagiarism, but not exactly original: the Rolling Stones' debut album cover was seen as a nod in the direction of the *With The Beatles* sleeve, which had been released not long before. In more recent years, a straight parody of the Beatles' cover came with the release in 1977, on Stiff Records, of an EP by London pub band Roogalator called simply *With The Roogalator*. This imitated not only the photographic concept, but also retained the typography of the original. Similarly, a 1984 collection of early '60s Liverpool groups aped the design, substituting the faces with four actual mop-heads.

A pastiche of the whole Beatles phenomenon appeared on British television screens in 1978, an offshoot of the *Rutland Weekend Television* programme called the Rutles. The brainchild of Monty Python's Eric Idle, with music by humourist/musician Neil Innes (who also played the John Lennon character in the "pre-fab four"),

Cover of *Liverpool Beat: Vol. 2*, 1984.

**meet
the
rutles**

stereo

Tragical History Tour
The fool On The pill   Lying   Blue day Way
Your Mother Should Go   I Am The Waitress

RUTLES

TRAGICAL HISTORY
TOUR

Includes 24-page full color picture book

hello Get lost   ✠✗✗   W.C. fields forever
Denny Lane Abie You're A Rich Man
All You Need Is lunch

**SGT RUTTERS
DARTS CLUB BAND**

RUTLES

LET IT ROT

National Lampoon: Pages from the "Beatles Edition", October 1977.

the Rutles became an album, with tracks that unnervingly parodied the varying styles and idiosyncracies of the Beatles; and the TV film itself did the same, equally brilliantly, on a visual level. As if to give some "seal of approval" to the venture, George Harrison actually appeared in the film, a prelude to his closer involvement in the production of Python-based films.

A distinctly American send-up of the Beatles came with a whole edition of *National Lampoon* magazine devoted to the group in 1978. While much centred on sex-oriented jokes concerning Beatles fans rather than the group and its history, parodies of specific album designs and their general style abounded. Examples of the latter included, in an "unreleased albums" section, Paul McCartney's "return to his roots" in a joint LP with Frank Sinatra, and the *Little Red Album* (shades of the "white album" and Mao Tse Tung's *Little Red Book*) which contained such unknown Beatles gems as *Love Mao Do*, *Rice Paddies Forever*, *Paperback Tiger* and *Happiness Proceeds*

Out Of The Barrel Of A Gun. Album sleeve parodies in the Lampoon special included the Beatles, complete with orthodox Jewish hats and hairlocks, on *Rabbi Soul* (a pun reminiscent of a 1964 US novelty single by the Bagels *I Want To Hold Your Hair*), and, on the cover of the magazine, the Abbey Road crossing with the Beatles squashed flat like gingerbread men, a road roller chugging into the distance.

Abbey road has proved as popular an image as any for imitation and parody. As recently as 1982 Solid State Logic commissioned illustrator Adrian Chesterman to paint the crossing, one side of the road as it appears on the album, the other full of futuristic buildings and vehicles; the Beatles are faint ghosts on the zebra crossing while in the foreground is the company's latest piece of recording mixer-desk technology. A copy of the work hangs in studio manager Ken Townshend's office at Abbey Road, the original in the Solid State studios in rural Oxfordshire.

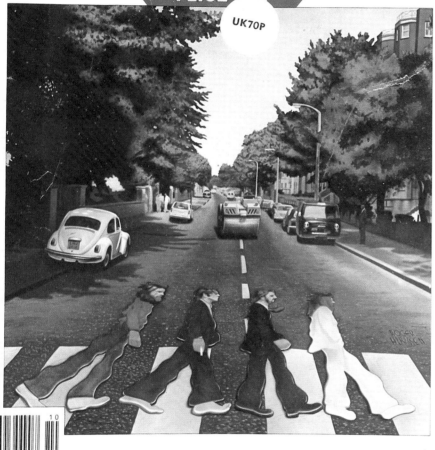

Adrian Chesterman: Painting commissioned for an advertisement for Solid State Logic, 1982.

Hipgnosis: "Beatlemania".

It Was Twenty Years Ago Today

The most straightforward exploitation of the nostalgia factor has been in the area of fan memorabilia and, in recent years, in the celebration of various Beatles anniversaries. It is here that the Beatles images of the '60s have most been perpetuated in their original form without the modification of either parody or artistic adaptation.

An important aspect of this has been the market in Beatles posters. The general fashion for posters has subsided since the early '70s, but, nevertheless, every conceivable image that constituted part of the visual legacy of the Beatles has been blown up to poster size. Photographs that were originally published as postcards now hang crown-size in fans' bedrooms; record sleeve art and book covers, movie adverts and straight newspaper pictures, have all been borrowed or plagiarised by the poster manufacturers. There has been some recycling of posters that were intended that way in the first place – Hoffmann's "on the beach" shot, which was marketed on its first appearance in 1963 by *Reveille* magazine, Avedon's "psychedelic" pictures – but since them, there has been little original poster design concerning the Beatles.

What there has been of interest has seemed to come as the by-product of some more ambitious project. A map of Liverpool pin-pointing all the places of interest to Beatles enthusiasts (birthplaces, schools, venues and so on) was published by the City of Liverpool Public Relations Office in 1974 as part of a Beatles package aimed at tourists and Beatles fans generally. The kit, entitled *The Beatles Collection* also included a blow-by-blow account of their career done as a poster, and a replica of the last ever newsletter from the official Beatles Fan Club to its members in early 1972, in the name of Freda Kelly who had been secretary at its Liverpool branch since its inception in 1962. (Interestingly, the fan club logo retained Tex O'Hara's original drumskin design with the beetle's antennae forming part of the B, while the Beatles silhouette, which also featured on the letterhead, has

persisted on the notepaper of the Japanese Beatles Fan Club, now the largest organisation of its kind in the world.)

EMI records celebrated the 20th anniversary of the Beatles' first record release with a "Twenty Years Ago" campaign which included a set of four posters ("Did you know that George Harrison used to be in a group called the Beatles...?" etc) that actually functioned as such on billboards, in record shops, and even on London buses. The campaign carried the logo – yet again an adaptation of a Dezo Hoffmann picture – onto t-shirts, badges and stickers, all accompanying the relaunch of their singles as picture discs on the anniversary of the original release of each one.

One of the most original posters to come out of post-Beatles Beatlemania was in fact entitled *Beatlemania*. Originally part of a publicity package for a Thames Television series that never materialised, the photograph, by design company Hipgnosis, was subsequently published as a poster by a Dutch-based company. It depicted simply a bus queue of schoolgirls in various stages of realisation that the Beatles are passing by in a car. The Beatles themselves appear not at all – the only clue is the *Beatles Monthly* magazine being read by the girl at the head of the line – but the photograph succeeds in encapsulating the entire experience of Beatlemania; from ignorance to dawning recognition to amazement, euphoria and, finally hysteria. Hipgnosis were, in fact, responsible for some of the most spectacular rock illustration in the '70s and early '80s, primarily on record sleeves.

Where Beatles fan activity has been most concentrated in recent years has been at the "conventions" held worldwide, where all manner of memorabilia and ephemera abounds, sometimes original but more often replicas. These events also involve lectures, film shows, and "Beatles Brain" quizzes, but they are dominated by the marketing in every way imaginable of every aspect of the Beatles' image. In many ways, these extravaganzas – held as far apart as Liverpool and San Francisco, Amsterdam and Tokyo, are the most conspicuous

manifestation of the continuing fascination of the group. The extent of this fascination can even be measured in hard cash. Within the refined portals of Sotheby's, in the art and antique sale rooms, a "rock'n'roll memorabilia" auction is held annually, an event dominated by Beatles material. As well as "personal" objects – drawings by John, a jacket of Paul's, Ringo's drumsticks and suchlike – a large number of the objects on sale are '60s trivia, now collectors items, the Beatles' stamp giving almost anything a market price astronomical in relation to its original cost.

Commemorative in a more permanent sense, but definitely a response to the post-Beatles boom, has been the appearance (after a surprising absence in earlier years) of civic statues dedicated to the Beatles, primarily in their home town of Liverpool. Had Liverpool been in America, some piece of public sculpture of or for the Beatles would have appeared long before the group disbanded. Yet, even after their passing, it still took years of debate, petitions and pressure groups to convince the powers-that-be that Merseyside should have its own memorial to its four most famous sons.

What has eventually appeared has been less than satisfactory, and a result of private (rather than public – civic or municipal) patronage. The first memorial to appear was by Liverpool sculptor Arthur Dooley, unveiled by a local comedian and the Spinners folk group (!) in 1974. At that time, the site of the Cavern club in Mathew Street had been flattened, the wasteground being used as a car park, so the Dooley sculpture, dedicated to "Four Lads Who Shook The World" was on the wall of the warehouse opposite (where another club was briefly renamed the Cavern). As with most of Dooley's work over the previous decade, it featured a Madonna and child – or, more accurately, children – with the infants, claimed Dooley, representing the Beatles. Referring to one winged cherub, he explained at the time "That's Paul, the one with wings....." (an unfortunate remark in the light of a more recent schoolboy joke about what Paul McCartney and John Lennon have in common).

The most satisfactory piece of Beatles sculpture to appear in a public place in Liverpool was in fact a private donation from its creator, singer Tommy Steele. It consists of Eleanor Rigby sitting alone, an empty place next to her for passers by, a sad figure in busy Stanley Street.

On the actual site of the original Cavern club – in the Royal Life Cavern Walks development in Mathew Street – is a statue of the four Beatles by sculptor John Doubleday, unveiled in mid-1984. The target of much criticism that "it could be anybody", it forms the centrepiece of the complex, which houses shops, the Cavern Mecca Beatles Information Centre and a reopened Cavern club which is a direct replica (in fact one basement down) of the original. An interesting feature is the moulding on the facade of the Cavern Walks building (itself an impressive project by Liverpool architect David Backhouse), designed by Cynthia Lennon.

These "commercial" aspects of Beatle-oriented activity over the years since the break-up – books, records, plays, posters or fan club conventions – are far from being the full story. The Beatles' image had been recognised and used by "serious" artists – as "fine" art rather than commercial art – through the '60s, and just as the disbandment of the group led to an explosion in commercial art, so too, once they had become more than a merely temporary phenomenon, did the incorporation of the image into fine art accelerate. Just as pop subjects were adopted by pop artists some time after their establishment through the popular media, so has a high proportion of the "art of the Beatles" appeared over the past fifteen years, indeed much since – and no doubt stimulated by – the death of John Lennon.

Tommy Steele: The sculptor with "Eleanor Rigby" in Stanley Street, Liverpool.

Ron Jones

Memorabilia: including Sothebys' catalogue featuring a John Lennon Christmas card.

David Oxtoby: The apocalyptic "English Rock" (1976), later transformed into the tranquil "blue" version.

I Read The News Today, Oh Boy!

The demise of the Beatles coincided with the close of the '60s, the end of the "high" times, and the end of optimism and euphoria. Disillusionment set in as the economic recession began to bite, and the new young, the successors to the generation "liberated" by the affluence of the past decade, were the most conspicuous victims. Inflation and unemployment brought to an abrupt end the teenage economic miracle, and the surging youth culture that went with it.

The Beatles' break-up could be seen as their final contribution to the creation of new trends; dissolution, after all, was one of the keynotes of the forthcoming decade. That, of course, would be fanciful, but it is undeniable that their departure signalled the end of a dream, the decline of the cult of youth from something idealistic to something at best trivial and dull, at worst ugly and violent. The mere fact of the Beatles' existence, runnning chronologically "in tandem" with the "good" times, ending in timely fashion at the onset of the "bad", would have been enough to mark them as symbols of an era, even if their contribution to that era had been less fundamental than it was.

Before their final departure from the stage, the Beatles were already being viewed from a wider perspective. As the "swinging sixties" drew to a close, the writing was perceived on many a wall. The message of love and peace had become blurred in the haze of CS gas hanging over the streets of Paris in 1968, ignored at Kent State University where a student protester lay dead, forgotten as violence stalked the Altamont rock festival in front of the cameras and the Rolling Stones; the acid had begun to corrode, and the hang-over due to past over-indulgence began to set in. Things looked likely to get worse before they got better. Subconsciously, many sensed that the Beatles had no role in the new scenario, and began assessing their importance to the fast-fading world they had helped to create.

At one level, this made them objects of simple nostalgia, and provided the basis for the commercialisation of the Beatles' image. But at another level, it isolated them and turned them into symbols of the attitudes as much as the era of the '60s. The artist could thus legitimately use them to personify the whole of the '60s *gestalt*, much as an earlier generation might have used Virgil to represent the classical era or Romeo and Juliet the tragedy of blighted love. The symbol was not always the Beatles as a group, nor even the separate individuals in their collective heyday; often they were portrayed as they became in the years after the break-up when, for the first time in their adult lives, they assumed truly individual roles. But it was always their past as Beatles that remained the essence.

David Oxtoby: "English Rock" (2).

When I Get Older, Losing My Hair

David Oxtoby

David Oxtoby: "Yesterdays With Blue Guitar", 1978.

David Oxtoby came to prominence in the mid-'70s as the foremost among painters specialising in subjects drawn from the world of popular musicians. His success was marked in 1978 by the publication of his work in book form, *Oxtoby's Rockers*. Until 1984, he had only painted the Beatles as individuals – John Lennon and Paul McCartney.

Oxtoby was born in 1938, and attended Bradford College of Art where he was part of the group that included Norman Stevens, John Loker, Michael Vaughan and David Hockney. He specialised in illustrative homages to his own teenage heroes; rock'n'roll heroes in the main – Elvis, Buddy Holly, Eddie Cochran *et al* – against the backgrounds and symbols of their own self-made mythologies. But he also painted contemporary personalities from the world of rock music, and it was in this context that Lennon and McCartney figured in his work.

His *English Rock* in its original 1976 form no longer exists. Depicting John Lennon wearing his familiar New York City t-shirt against a blazing metropolis, he subsequently changed it to a version with a more serene blue background. Oxtoby has enjoyed extensive patronage in the world of rock music, and the revised version of *English Rock* is now the property of Elton John's manager, John Reid. Oxtoby now sees the original as being prophetic in the light of Lennon's death – "…the destruction in New York…and even the shadow in the window…in retrospect you could say it was a coffin image, with the crucifix and all.."

Paul McCartney as superstar with Wings was the subject of Oxtoby's other '70s Beatles portrait, yet (even in the title) reference was still being made to the undeniable past, of both subject and artist – "*Yesterdays With Blue Guitar* is a combination drawing of Paul with my yesterdays. The background contains drawings based on the works of many of my friends while badges scattered across Paul's chest have names of other friends. The drawing was born out of a conversation with David Hockney who told me he was working on a series of etchings based on a poem inspired by a Picasso painting. I figured one thing missing from that sequence was a drawing!" (From *Oxtoby's Rockers*, 1978)

Mull of Kintyre, Paul McCartney's most overtly commercial record of his post-Beatles output – and inevitably most successful – provided the subject for Oxtoby's pun-laden *Wing Commander And The Apple Corps*. McCartney appears as a ghost-like presence on the blue background (again the past haunting the present?) behind a Scots piper in full regalia – regalia which includes, on closer inspection, the badge of the Apple Corps; an apple core!

An artist noted specifically for his work with Paul McCartney is Humphrey Ocean. During the early '70s, Ocean was a member of the London rock group Kilburn and the High Roads, an ex-art school band which was the nucleus for Ian Dury and the Blockheads; he became involved with McCartney after doing the artwork for the inner sleeve of *Wings At The Speed Of Sound*. This led directly to his engagement as "artist in residence" to accompany McCartney's group on their American tour of 1976, the results of which were

James Hall Thomson

David Oxtoby: "Wing Commander And The Apple Corps", 1983.

David Oxtoby

published in the book of drawings and paintings *The Ocean View*. His portrait of Paul McCartney himself was commissioned after he had won first prize in the third of the annual Imperial Tobacco Exhibitions held at the National Portrait Gallery.

Cartoonists, with their eyes trained to capture the personality behind the mask, were also sensitive to the changing characters of the individual Beatles, and documented their emerging solo persona through the '70s. A good example can be seen in the work of Jimmy Thomson, whose bold portraits of the major names in rock music adorned the pages of *Melody Maker* from the 1960s onwards. His pictures of the Beatles over the years reflect their changing image until well into the '70s, when they were considered by all – despite their efforts to the contrary – as "ex-Beatles".

The world renowned cartoonist Al Hirschfeld, famous since the 1930s for his work on the theatre pages of the Sunday edition of the *New York Times*, produced a portrait of a post-Beatles Ringo

Starr in the early 1970s. Whether or not Ringo was the only Beatle he drew is not clear, but right up to the end of (and after) the group's career, Ringo occupied a special place in America's affection for the Beatles, which would explain the master's choice. The drawing itself was not typical of Hirschfield's style, the usual almost angular art-deco style of portraiture having given way to a more leisurely fluid approach.

Apart from this, Ringo as an individual subject appeared in little artwork over the years. Although the Beatles were invariably treated as equals in group illustrations during their cooperative years, the same is not true of their solo images, in which John and Paul undoubtedly dominated. George Harrison in particular has seldom been singled out for special treatment, although, of course, photographic portraits and paintings of him as part of the group are plentiful. This is, in some ways, surprising.

George emerged towards the end of the group's career as a songwriter of great merit, not just as lead guitar to the composing talents of Lennon and McCartney, and he confirmed his stature in his later solo career. Furthermore, his influence on the artistic direction of the Beatles was crucial in his adoption of Eastern musical forms – both in his songs and in the use of the sitar. It was George who sparked the group's interest in the philosophy and practise of meditation, and although their association with the Maharishi was short-lived, the broader effects were to be apparent in the Beatles' musical output, in varying degrees, until their disbandment. George was at least a contributory factor in the cult of eastern mysticism in'60s cultural orthodoxy, and directly responsible for an important aspect of the Beatles' image after 1967.

Harrison, of course, has always appeared more of a recluse, more introverted, than the rest of the group; and despite his actively creative interests in film production and ornamental gardening, the impression has remained. It is no doubt this that has led to his being the least "conspicuous" of the group – both before and since the death of John Lennon – in terms of individual profiles of the various ex-Beatles.

Jimmy Thomson: cartoons from *Melody Maker*.

And Now These Days Are Gone

ndividual portraits apart, art featuring the Beatles since 1970 has broadly fallen into two categories, with two different aims: it has been used to symbolise the '60s; or it has been purely representational. The dividing line between these two is not always clear. Any picture of the Beatles is likely to evoke the era of which they were a part, and which they influenced so profoundly, whether that is the artist's intention or not. Conversely, a '60s evocation using the Beatles as a symbol can easily be interpreted as a straight portrait of the group. The functions are interchangeable. The Beatles' image has come to be factual/nostalgic/mythical/symbolic, depending on the perspective from which it is viewed. Its popularity, its universality, is rooted in this versatility; it does for us what we wish it to do. Once manipulated by commerce, status, and sheer adulation, the Beatles' image is now manipulated by the solitary consumer, free to fulfil his or her own needs. Now they are no more, the Beatles'

collective face is truly common property.

A case in point. As part of a Jubilee Year (1977) competition, the insurance company Alexander Howden commissioned Liverpool painter Maurice Cockrill to illustrate an aspect of British success over the previous twenty-five years. Subjects included sport, technology and so on. The Beatles were to represent the Arts – not just pop music, or music generally, but the whole of contemporary art. Unlike David Oxtoby, Cockrill did not paint pictures of the famous before his Beatles portraits. Born in 1936, he had moved to Liverpool from North Wales in the early '60s and by the late '60s his work was in the then emergent photo-realist style, dominated by urban landscapes – or, to be more exact, suburban landscapes – neat rows of foliage against the clean lines of walls and buildings.

Using a photograph of the Beatles by Don McCullin, Cockrill placed the four portraits – as though torn from the photograph – above a Penny Lane street sign, the inevitable green hedge in the background. The sign itself bears the graffiti of girls' names – Jude, Lucy, Rita, Michelle – the eponymous heroines of Beatles' songs.

The painting, *Penny Lane*, works at several different levels. Its main function, and the reason why it was commissioned in the first place, is to commemorate and encapsulate a past artistic triumph. On the other hand, when used by Merseyside County Council as a best-selling postcard and as the cover for a local guidebook *In The Footsteps Of The Beatles*, it served primarily to evoke a particular location, a geographical area, in terms of its association with the Beatles. Finally, it remains Cockrill's personal vision of the Beatles, the jagged edges of the torn up photograph suggestive of the pains of separation and the impossibility of repair, and the whole painting reminiscent of a casually discarded memento of the past. *Penny Lane* has become an important part of the latter-day imagery of the Beatles.

An enigmatic portrayal of the Beatles as a group – perhaps no more than a visual pun – came from

Maurice Cockrill: "Penny Lane", 1977.

Maurice Cockrill/Alexander Howden

the hand of surrealist pioneer Max Ernst, who died in 1975. Ernst, who had been living in the United States for some years, depicted the group as four insects, their bodies being constructed from what appear to be percussive musical instruments.

Another wry and rather oblique comment came from John Cornelius, the Liverpool artist and musician. Cornelius earned a living for some time drawing portraits in Liverpool 8 clubland, and recorded his reflections on this and other aspects of Merseyside in *Liverpool 8*, published in the aftermath of the Toxteth riots in 1982. In it he used a caricature of the Beatles to sum up a vanished aspect of the "swinging sixties"; captioned "In the 'sixties, all over Britain, it was the trendy thing to adopt a Scouse accent", the drawing was of four far from trendy looking youths. It was not so much a caricature of the Beatles as a caricature of the times they represented, thrown into relief by the very different circumstances of today.

It is far easier, of course, to use the Beatles as a comment on the '60s now that both are fifteen years in the past. Their own individual activities, even before Lennon's death, gradually distanced them from the legend – for legend it had become. But it was one event more than any other that set the seal on the legend, and ensured its perpetuation into the generations to come – the assassination of John Lennon.

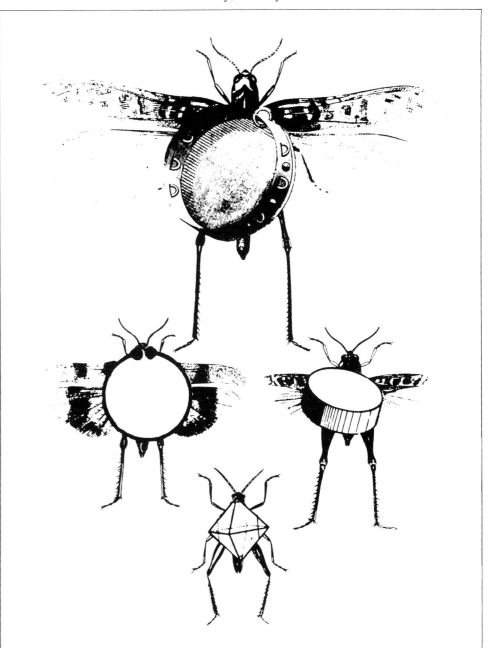

Max Ernst: "Beatles, 1969".

John Cornelius: "In the 'sixties all over Britain, it was the trendy thing to adopt a scouse accent". From *Liverpool 8* (John Murray, 1982).

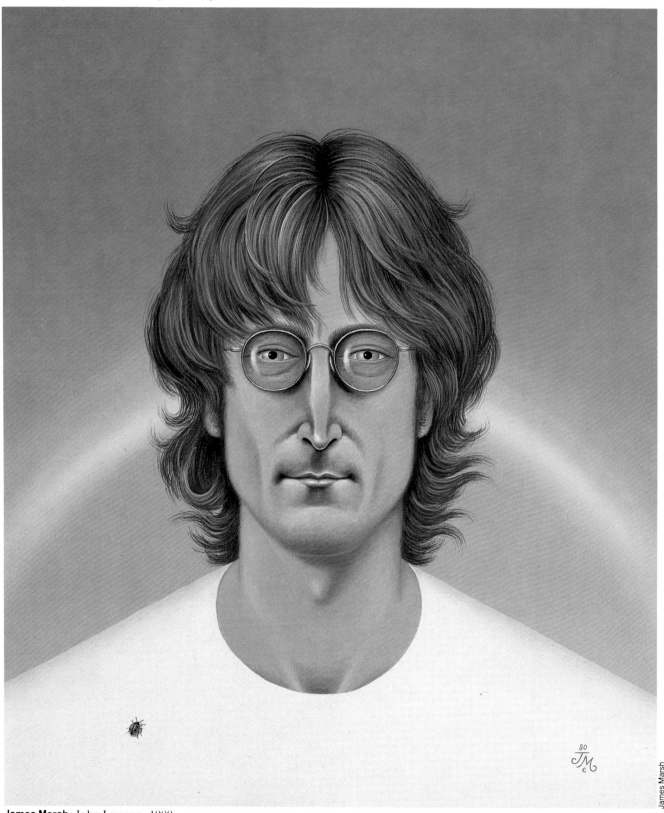

James Marsh: John Lennon, 1980.

Black Cloud Crossed My Mind, Blue Mist Round My Soul

The murder of John Lennon provided the stimulus for much of the art featuring the Beatles that appeared during the 1980s. The nostalgia that had undoubtedly inspired much of the post-Beatles activity in the visual arts and elsewhere was heightened by the death of the man who, perhaps more than any of the other three, epitomised the Beatles, even after their disbandment. Pictures of individual Beatles painted since 1980 have understandably been dominated by works dedicated to John Lennon.

The London illustrator, James Marsh, who had already painted a surreal portrait of Lennon in 1976 (originally for an article about fantasy and the imagination in the *Shell Times*) provided a further painting for an obituary piece in an American Magazine, *Northern Ohio Live*. Both were marked by Marsh's highly personal style, and included what appears to be something of a trademark – the various tiny insects which were also a feature of his subsequent cover artwork for Philip Norman's *Shout* (see page 108).

Most of the paintings that resulted from the Lennon tragedy were spontaneous gestures rather than specific commissions. However, although many could be said to be the work of "fans", this does not mean that all were of an amateur nature. Certainly, Beatles fan clubs, magazines and centres like Liverpool's Cavern Mecca were inundated with artistic endeavours of all kinds, but among the flood of dedications were works by full-time artists who happened to be fans as well.

A study of John Lennon and Yoko Ono by New York photographer Jack Mitchell, taken in the summer of 1980 only months before Lennon's death, was the basis for two such works that appeared in the wake of the Dakota Building shooting, works in very different media that nevertheless retained the basic image of the Mitchell portrait. One was by Hedva Kallech-Lederman, an Israeli painter specialising in acrylic painting on wood. Kallech-Lederman graduated at the London College of Printing in 1968 and worked for a time in New York before returning to Tel

James Marsh: "Imagination", 1976.

Hedva Kallech-Lederman: John Lennon, 1980.

Keith R. Jones: "One World: One People: John Ono Lennon", 1980.

Aviv, where she painted the Lennon portrait from the Mitchell photograph after it had appeared in *Time* magazine within a week of Lennon's death. The delicate painting on polished wood is truly icon-like, both in its choice of medium and in its pietistic quality.

Similarly, Cardiff-born New Jersey painter Keith R. Jones was moved to paint his *One World: One People: John Ono Lennon* soon after the death of Lennon, and used as a starting point the same Jack Mitchell photograph; but the results are totally different. Like the original, his painting includes Yoko next to John as an integral part of the composition. In Jones' own words: " I was so badly moved by the demise of John that I needed to come to terms with my feelings. I had to overcome the shock of anger and bitterness that surrounded his death. What transpired was a tribute to a man who championed the issue of peace, and fortunately I was able to complete the work without encumbering it with senseless negativity. John Ono-Lennon was, after all, positive in his drive for peace."

From a rather different perspective – that of an artist who was in Liverpool, indeed at Liverpool College Of Art, when the Beatles were playing at the Cavern – is the Lennon homage by sculptor and illustrator Franklin Wilson. Wilson studied art in Liverpool from 1960 to 1964 before entering the Royal College of Art in London. As an amateur drummer when a student at Liverpool, he can claim to have once lent his drumkit to John Lennon and Pete Best for an early Beatles gig. His windswept-hair-and-sideboards drawing of Lennon makes a striking and unusual image.

Much of the "fan" art is, inevitably, naive; '80s "living room" style brought to bear on a subject charged with emotional content – in fact the classic chemistry of kitsch. Not all of it can be dismissed so easily, however, as witness the remarkable set of cushions given to Cynthia Lennon by an American fan, Sharon Singer. The cushions were embroidered with various pictures of Cynthia and John taken from Cynthia's book *A Twist Of Lennon*, capturing the graphic quality of the originals in a unique way.

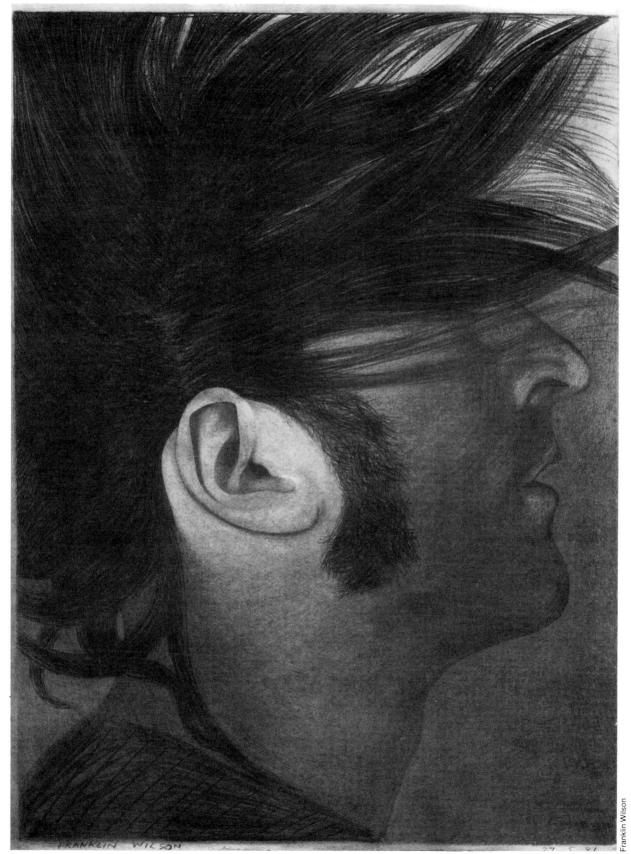

Franklin Wilson: John Lennon, 1980.

Franklin Wilson

J. Generalić: From 1973, painted on glass, this work from Yugoslavia represents a movement of untrained "naive" painters in the '70s who have since become commercially successful, several of whom used the Beatles as subject matter.

We Hope You Will Enjoy The Show

The Beatles' image is now a multi-faceted one. They will always be the lovable mop-tops *and* the Sgt Pepper band *and* Liverpool rockers. The effect of the passing of time has been to concertina the periods of change in the visual appearance of the Beatles so that they have become parts of one composite whole rather than chronologically separate events. It was this consideration that led directly to an exhibition devoted to the "art of the Beatles", and indirectly to this book.

The Beatles have been the most accessible, recognisable and at the same time prestigious of Liverpool's cultural exports. In 1984, in an effort to heal the painful emotional scars and material damage of the Toxteth riots of 1982, the city was designated the site of that year's International Garden Festival and a major exercise in rehabilitation was undertaken. As part of Merseyside's re-awakening pride in its own heritage, it seemed appropriate to devote an exhibition at Liverpool's well-known Walker Art Gallery to the very real effects that the Beatles have had on our visual environment.

The first task in the organisation of the exhibition was to locate sufficient material to make the whole project worth while. This exercise in itself unearthed works previously not widely known. The Japanese "hotel" painting by all four Beatles (see page 62) surfaced in this way, as did the Bratby portrait of Paul McCartney (page 74) and the David Wynne sculptures (page 46). The only references to the latter were press cuttings from the mid-'60s when the work was done. The Bratby painting came to light as an unsolicited offer for the exhibition on the part of the present owner.

Another gem that came to light was a large painting by Cynthia Lennon, the property of a children's hospital in Atlanta Georgia. In it, the Beatles are depicted as the dress-suited hoofers from their "Busby Berkeley" sequence (*Your Mother Should Know*) in *Magical Mystery Tour*. The painting, which dates from 1981, was the result of a specific commission from the hospital, and certainly – if only in size – contrasts sharply with Cynthia Lennon's better-known work. And one remarkable work came to light only days before the exhibition began, an eight foot canvas by a young Yorkshire artist, of which more later (see page 142).

Some ambitions for the exhibition remained unfulfilled, a major one being the reconstruction of the Sgt Pepper tableau; few of the objects proved traceable, or have even survived. On the other hand, items lost in the mists of time re-appeared, for example a Stuart Sutcliffe self-portrait, the painting of a bird by the eleven-year-old John Lennon, and a wooden sculpture of Ringo from 1962 by Tex O'Hara, the artist responsible for their "antennae" drumskin logo.

Tex O'Hara: The Beatles, 1962.

Cynthia Lennon: The Beatles, 1981.

David Oxtoby: "Yesterdays", 1984.

An important feature of the exhibition was the commissioning of a new work by David Oxtoby, to be used on the catalogue, poster and other publicity material for the event. Entitled *Yesterdays*, it was Oxtoby's first painting of the Beatles as a group, and made direct reference to the mop top days of *A Hard Day's Night*. Two closely related versions, using the same "frame" format but not the precise "Hard Day's Night" images, are called *I'm Looking Through You* and *You Won't See Me*.

What became clear during the assembling of the "Art of the Beatles" collection was the amount of straightforward portraiture of the Beatles that had appeared during the 1980s. One example was the work of a Liverpool painter under the pseudonym "Rod". Painted in 1981, it portrayed the Beatles as they were around 1969, and was seemingly based on the same McCullin photo' session as Maurice Cockrill's *Penny Lane* (Lennon all sideboards and granny glasses, George with swept back hair, Ringo moustached, Paul in open-neck shirt and jacket). It was titled, ironically, *Silver Beatles*. Paul Mason was another contemporary Merseyside painter represented, with a painting from 1982 which was almost certainly based on a picture from the same McCullin session.

Cockrill, meanwhile, had used the same image as in his *Penny Lane* for a reshuffled version of the torn up photograph (see front cover). This time a direct commission for Merseyside Tourism in 1981, *Strawberry Fields* had the pictures scattered on fallen leaves set against the gothic gates of Strawberry Field – entrance to a fantasy landscape of sculptured trees, far removed from the crumbling reality of Lennon's childhood, recalled in the Beatles' classic song.

As well as painting, photography, sculpture and so on, the "Art of the Beatles" exhibition was able to embrace some works executed in more unusual media. A mixed-media "assemblage" by ex-Liverpool Art College student Sue Butler, *Dear Diary*, consisted of the tangible memoirs of teenage days in the Cavern – a satchel with a copy of *Merseybeat* sticking out between exercise books and exam papers, black woollen scarf and membership card, evidence of lunchtime "sagging" from school. And Rod Murray, one time flatmate and fellow student of Lennon and Sutcliffe, and now a lecturer in the Fine Art department at the College, contributed one of the more significant exhibits in terms of the art of the Beatles to come – a hologram of the Yellow Submarine.

The Art of the Beatles exhibition demonstrated

"Rod": "Silver Beatles", 1981.

Maurice Cockrill: "Strawberry Fields", 1981.

unequivocally the extent to which the image of the Beatles has become a permanent part of our visual vocabulary. It is a vocabulary that has been much enriched by innovations during the '60s in graphics, photography, painting, animation, and other areas of the visual arts, and they were innovations in which the Beatles were often closely involved – as instigators by example or sometimes as patrons. But it is the group's own image that remains the most potent visual legacy of the '60s; its ubiquity in the '80s shows that it has lost none of its power.

As Far As The Eye Can See

The image of the Beatles appeals to the romantic in all of us, linked indissolubly to a musical legacy that has come to represent eight years in many of our lives: for those still in their early thirties, a quarter of their entire lives, the all important years of adolescence, to which the Beatles provided the soundtrack. For those of the same generation as the Beatles, now in their forties, there was an affinity born of common roots and cultural reference; for them the Beatles created an extended youth – to be young in the '60s was not the prerogative of just the under-twenties any more. And a new generation, only now in their twenties or even their 'teens (the latter being born as the Beatles were breaking up) has also inherited the music, but their image of the Beatles is based entirely on received impressions. They have a view of the Beatles that those older among us will never be completely able to appreciate – we, to some degree or another, were *there* when the songs were part of our lives and they were new, and the image was flesh too, however remote the reality.

The romantic element in the image of the Beatles is parallel to that in their music, isolating and idealising aspects of reality but, in doing so, actually making the reality that much richer. Love songs articulate emotions by simplifying them, and in consequence both heighten their impact and enable them to be recollected with accuracy.

That the Beatles – specifically Lennon and McCartney – were heirs to the romantic mantle goes without saying. They were undoubtedly the finest songwriters in the romantic tradition to emerge in the post-war years. This is true not just of the love songs, but of the recollections of childhood in *Penny Lane* or *Strawberry Fields*, the fantasy landscapes of *Lucy In The Sky* and *Fool On The Hill*, homages to their own musical roots (Chuck Berry in *Back In The USSR*, Little Richard in *I'm Down* and so on), affectionate nods to collective nostalgia with *When I'm Sixty-four* and *Your Mother Should Know*, and the isolated and idealised figures of Eleanor Rigby and Lovely Rita and the rest of them drawn from the urban

landscape – all are interpreted with that "visionary gleam" that Wordsworth identified as the perspective, the sense of wonder, of childhood. All their songs, regardless of subject matter, were catalysts in the cultural explosion of the period.

The same can be said of the image of the Beatles; it provided the visual dimension to the impact of the Beatles, their impact on *style* as much as on art. Most of those who incorporated the Beatles into their work in some way or another were part of a modern day continuation of the romantic tradition. Stuart Sutcliffe himself was the archetypal late-'50s bohemian, his Beatles activity a romantic role in itself. Certainly Adrian Henri would agree to the "romantic" description; and Peter Blake, Maurice Cockrill and David Oxtoby all treated their Beatles subject matter with the same affection, the same glowing enthusiasm, as the Beatles did their song subject matter.

This similarity of approach – the Beatles to their very "visual" lyrics and the visual artists to their own work – is another essential element in the affinity that painters and artists felt with the Beatles. They were not just a ready-made image or symbol for the '60s, but "literary" creators of potent visual power, albeit not visual artists.

The visitor to Liverpool is – for the first time since their rise to fame in 1963 – made very aware that it is the bithplace of the Beatles. Permanent reminders, all recent innovations, include the Beatle City "experience" tracing the group's history, and the Cavern walks development in Mathew Street which houses a reopened Cavern club as well as the Cavern Mecca Beatles Information Centre and the "Abbey Road" pub. Also in Mathew Street is a Beatles souvenir shop, and the dubiously conceived John Lennon Memorial Club, an after-hours drinking club which has "Give Peace A Chance" emblazoned above the bar. Throughout these manifestations of the city's long-overdue realisation of its heritage – or at least of the stimulus to do something about it – run adaptations of the most enduring, most commonly accepted, pictures of the Beatles. As with their use over the years on a world-wide basis, it would be hard to say how many of these adaptations are "official", but the constant repetition, with occasional modification, of these classic images of the Beatles ensures their continued place in the popular consciousness, and consequently in the work of visual artists of all kinds.

One such work, which utilised not just one but virtually *all* the images of the Beatles that have become common currency, came to light during the final days before the Art of the Beatles exhibition. By a part-time Yorkshire painter Barry Agar, it is a truly remarkable eight-foot long canvas depicting the Beatles, in the form of a collage, at every stage of their career. At first sight the work appear to be an actual collage, so exactly are the scores of photographs reproduced; but the entire work was painted by Agar over a period of two years. It follows chronologically – like some Bayeaux tapestry of the Beatles – the development of the Beatles' image, from the black-and-white memories of Hamburg and Liverpool, through the years of Beatlemania and the rainbow days of psychedelia, to the final pictures linked with *Abbey Road* and *Let It Be*.

In many ways the painting summarises what the Art of the Beatles is all about, both in content and in style; in content because it documents the changing faces of the Beatles while demonstrating the essential continuity that lay beneath; and in style because it is an adaptation, a modification, of those images to achieve a personal statement.

Agar's title – *The Trojan Horse* – hints that his intention is more than just a mural-sized montage of famous photographs; it is at one and the same time a homage, an evocation of the Beatles and their era, and an expression of the kaleidoscope of clearly defined impressions – not fading memories – that go to make up the collective image of the Beatles, the "Trojan horse" that invaded all our lives.

It has been said that the most universally recognised symbols of the 20th century have been the Coca Cola logo and the swastika – images so well known, so much a part of global culture, that they can be identified by *all*, save the most remote of primitive tribes. In human terms, we might add Charlie Chaplin, Adolf Hitler and Chairman Mao to the list; and the Beatles, along with Marilyn Monroe and Elvis Presley, could also be said to belong to this select category.

The Beatles arrived at the dawn of the greatest era of mass communication known to man, the birth of the "global village". As a result they became the universal symbol for that generation, and for the now often-ridiculed '60s ideals of optimism and (sometimes naive) enthusiasm, liberally laced with "love" in the broadest sense of the word. The continued recycling of the Beatles image is only partly pure nostalgia; some of it has to do with a genuine yearning for the ideals and hopes of the '60s and a desire to keep them, at least symbolically, alive.

Asked whether they were mods or rockers, Lennon once replied: "Neither – we're mockers" and he was right in more ways than one. This self-effacing attitude and the element of ridicule that accompanied it, is apparent in the two dimensional image of the Beatles time and time again, and who are we to argue? The worst thing we can do is to rationalise and analyse the Beatles' image – as certain musicologists have their songs – with a serious approach that negates the sense of humour running through all they did.

Plaque: Sean O'Halligan/photograph: Peter O'Halligan

Mathew Street, Liverpool, 1976.

Despite the quality of their work, the historic place it has in our culture, and their treatment during the '60s as near-deity, they always insisted that they were "just a band who made it very big". A decade and a half later, the scope and enduring quality of the image and the art surrounding the Beatles, demonstrates just how big that really was.

Barry Agar: "The Trojan Horse".

Index of Artists and Authors